# Prayers

and Heavenly Promises

**Compiled from Approved Sources**
**By Joan Carroll Cruz**

*8-15-06*

*Enjoy - Mommie*

# PRAYERS
## AND
# HEAVENLY PROMISES

*"I am Eternal Truth, incapable of any lie.
I am faithful to My promises."*
—Our Lord to St. Margaret Mary

*Holy Mary, Mother of God,*
*pray for us!*

# PRAYERS
## AND
# HEAVENLY PROMISES

Compiled from Approved Sources
by Joan Carroll Cruz

*"Ask, and it shall be given you: seek, and
you shall find: knock, and it shall be opened
to you. For every one that asketh, receiveth:
and he that seeketh, findeth: and to him that
knocketh, it shall be opened."*
—Matthew 7:7-8

TAN BOOKS AND PUBLISHERS, INC.
Rockford, Illinois 61105

Nihil Obstat:     Rev. Terry Tekippe
                  Censor Librorum

Imprimatur:    ✠ Most Rev. Francis B. Schulte
                  Archbishop of New Orleans
                  December 29, 1989

The Nihil Obstat and Imprimatur are the Church's declarations that a work is free from error in matters of faith and morals and in no way implies that the Church agrees with the contents of the book.

Nothing in this book should be read as implying that if a certain prayer is performed in a particular manner, a certain result will occur. The promises referred to in this work should be looked upon as manifestations of divine generosity and as encouragement to an even more devout life.

Library of Congress Catalog Card No.: 90-70225

ISBN: 0-89555-397-X

Printed and bound in the United States of America.


TAN BOOKS AND PUBLISHERS, INC.
P.O. Box 424
Rockford, Illinois 61105

1990

## A Powerful Prayer
## To Be Said Before Praying

"ALMIGHTY Father,
I place the Precious Blood of Jesus
before my lips before I pray,
that my prayers may be purified
before they ascend
to Your divine altar."

—*St. Mary Magdalen de Pazzi*

# Contents

# PRAYERS
AND
# HEAVENLY PROMISES

*"Everything I say to one of My children is for all of them . . . Each soul is My favorite . . . If only you knew My love for each one."*
—Our Lord to Gabrielle Bossis
(1874–1950)

# Morning Prayers

## A Morning Prayer based on Three Revelations of Our Lord

DEAR LORD, I adore Your Sacred Heart, which I desire to enter with acts of love, praise, adoration and thanksgiving. I offer You my own heart as I sigh to You from its very depths, asking that You will work through me in all that I do this day; thus may I draw You closer to me than You were before. I offer You all the crosses and sufferings of the world, in union with Your life on earth, in expiation for sins. Please join my every action and heartbeat to the pulsations of Your heart. I unite all my works of this day to those labors You performed while You were on earth, bathing them in Your precious Blood, and I offer them to the Heavenly Father so that many souls may be saved. Amen.

*This prayer is based on the following revelations:*

"When you awake, enter at once into My Heart, and when you are in it, offer My Father all your actions united to the pulsations of My Heart...If [a person is] engaged in work of no value in itself, if she bathes it in My Blood or unites

it to the work I Myself did during My mortal life, it will greatly profit souls...more, perhaps, than if she had preached to the whole world. You will be able to save many souls that way."
—*Our Lord to Sr. Josefa Menendez (1890-1923)*

"When you awake in the morning, let your first act be to salute My Heart, and to offer Me your own...Whoever shall breathe a sigh toward Me from the bottom of his heart when he awakes in the morning and shall ask Me to work all his works in him throughout the day, will draw Me to him...For never does a man breathe a sigh of longing aspiration toward Me without drawing Me nearer to him than I was before."
—*Our Lord to St. Mechtilde (1241-1298)*

"It is not merely by praying that souls are saved, but through the actions of even the most ordinary lives lived for God... Offer Me everything united to My life on earth...Offer Me all the crosses of the world. There are so many, and few think of offering them to Me in expiation for sins..."
—*Our Lord to Gabrielle Bossis (1874-1950)*

### Fatima Morning Offering
*(Based on Our Lady of Fatima's requests)*

O JESUS, through the Immaculate Heart of Mary, I offer You my prayers, works, joys and sufferings, all that this day may bring, be they good or bad: for the love of God, for the conversion of sinners, and in reparation for all the sins committed against the Sacred Heart of Jesus and the Immaculate Heart of Mary.

## Morning Offering to the Sacred Heart

O JESUS, through the Immaculate Heart of Mary, I offer You my prayers, works, joys and sufferings of this day for all the intentions of Your Sacred Heart, in union with the Holy Sacrifice of the Mass throughout the world, in reparation for my sins, for the intentions of all our associates, and in particular for the intentions of our Holy Father for this month.

—*The Apostleship of Prayer*

*Sheppard*

The Sacred Heart of Jesus

## ~ 2 ~

## 𝔑𝔦𝔤𝔥𝔱 𝔓𝔯𝔞𝔶𝔢𝔯𝔰

### Prayer for Daily Neglects

ETERNAL FATHER, I offer You the Sacred Heart of Jesus, with all its love, all its sufferings and all its merits.

First: To expiate all the sins I have committed this day and during all my life. *Glory be to the Father,* etc.

Second: To purify the good I have done poorly this day and during all my life. *Glory be to the Father,* etc.

Third: To supply for the good I ought to have done, and that I have neglected this day and all my life. *Glory be to the Father,* etc.

HISTORY: Soon after the death of a certain Poor Clare nun, she appeared to her abbess, who was praying for her, and said: "I went straight to Heaven because I paid all my debts by virtue of this prayer."

✝

## Night Prayer in Response
## to a Request from Our Lord

ETERNAL FATHER, I desire to rest in Your Heart this night. I make the intention of offering to You every beat of my heart, joining to them as many acts of love and desire. I pray that even while I am asleep, I will bring back to You souls that offend You. I ask forgiveness for the whole world, especially for those who know You and yet sin. I offer to You my every breath and heartbeat as a prayer of reparation. Amen.

"During the night you will rest in My Heart! My Heart will listen to the beats of yours, which will be so many acts of love and desire. Thus even while you are sleeping, you will bring back to Me souls that so offend Me. . .Ask forgiveness for the whole world, especially for those that know Me and yet sin; offer yourself in reparation!"

—*Our Lord to Sr. Josefa Menendez*

✝

"You were wondering how to use those moments when you wake up in the night. Speak to Me of love, ardently desiring your next Communion. . .Call Me by the gentlest names, even when you are half asleep. . ." —*Our Lord to Gabrielle Bossis*

✝

## Watch, O Lord

WATCH, O Lord, with those who wake, or watch, or weep tonight, and give Your angels and saints charge over those who sleep.

Tend Your sick ones, O Lord Christ.

Rest Your weary ones.

Bless Your dying ones.

Soothe Your suffering ones.

Pity Your afflicted ones.

Shield Your joyous ones,

and all for Your love's sake. Amen.

—*St. Augustine*

St. Augustine with Our Lady and the Christ Child.

# 3

# Mass and Holy Communion

## Preparation for Holy Communion

DEAR JESUS, I ardently desire to receive You. The moment draws near, the rapturous moment, in which I shall receive You, my God, into my soul. I come to You, I run to meet You with the utmost devotion and reverence of which I, as a little child, am capable. Stretch forth Your most sacred hands to embrace my soul—Your pierced hands which were stretched forth amid the anguish of Your Passion to embrace all sinners. I stretch forth not only my hands, but my heart and my soul, to embrace You and to lead You into the innermost and secret recess of my heart.

Would that I had within me as great a devotion, love and purity as You have ever been adored with by the heart of any mortal. Would that I were filled with all virtues, with all holy desires, with perfect devotion. Would that I had the purity of all Your angels, the charity of all Your apostles, the holiness of all confessors, the chastity and cleanness of heart of all virgins and the holy fire of love of all the martyrs. Would that I could receive You now with all that devotion, reverence and love with which Your most Blessed Mother received You in Your Incarnation, and in Your adorable Eucharist! Would that I had Your own sacred and divine Heart, that I might receive You as Your ineffable Majesty deserves!

I offer You, my sweetest Jesus—to be my fitting preparation, to make amends for all my unworthiness, my negligences, my lack of preparation, devotion and affections—I offer You the love which the Saints and the Blessed Mother had when they received You in this Holy Sacrament.

I offer You, most holy Jesus, Your own meritorious Heart, and all the ineffable virtues and graces which the most Blessed Trinity bestowed without measure upon it, that all my vileness and all my unworthiness may be covered, and that a proper and most peaceful abode may be prepared for You in my soul. Amen.

—*Author unknown*

PROMISE: "When you approach to receive Me in Holy Communion, receive Me with these intentions of feeling all the glowing desire and love with which the heart of any mortal has ever been inflamed. I will accept this love and preparation, not as it is in you, but what you desire your love and preparation to be."          —*Our Lord to the author of the above prayer*

✝

# The **Anima Christi** *or* **Soul of Christ**

*Traditionally prayed after Holy Communion*

SOUL of Christ, sanctify me.
Body of Christ, save me.
Blood of Christ, inebriate me.
Water from the side of Christ, wash me.
Passion of Christ, strengthen me.
O good Jesus, hear me.
Within Thy wounds, hide me.
Never let me be separated from Thee.
From the malignant enemy, defend me.
At the hour of my death, call me.
And bid me come unto Thee.
That with Thy saints I may praise Thee,
    forever and ever. Amen.

—*Enchiridion of Indulgences*

✝

WORDS OF THE SAINTS ON
THE IMMENSE VALUE OF HOLY MASS

"One single Mass gives more honor to God than all the
penances of the Saints, the labors of the Apostles, the sufferings of the martyrs and even the burning love of the Blessed
Mother of God." —*St. Alphonsus Liguori*

"The offering up of the Holy Mass benefits not only the
saints for whom [in whose honor] it is said, but the whole
Church of God in Heaven, on earth and in Purgatory."
—*St. John Vianney, The Curé of Ars*

"Put all the good works in the world against one Holy Mass; they will be as a grain of sand beside a mountain."

—*St. John Vianney, The Curé of Ars*

✝

Our Lord revealed to St. Gertrude that each time we look at the Most Blessed Sacrament with love, our place in Heaven is raised forever.

✝

## THE DEVOTION OF ST. BENEDICT JOSEPH LABRE

After receiving Holy Communion, it was the practice of St. Benedict Joseph Labre to offer to God all the loving aspirations of the Blessed Virgin Mary and the Apostles and Saints which they had made after they had received the Holy Eucharist.

✝

*Our Lady revealed to Ven. Mary of Agreda that in Heaven:*

"Those who had devoutly received Holy Communion will bear on their breast, where they have so often harbored the Holy Eucharist, most beautiful and resplendent inscriptions, showing that they were most worthy tabernacles of the Holy Sacrament . . . Moreover, the essential glory of those who have worthily and devoutly received the Holy Eucharist will, in several respects, exceed the glory of many martyrs who have not received the Body and Blood of the Lord."

## Prayer before a Crucifix
*Traditionally prayed after Holy Communion*

BEHOLD, O kind and most sweet Jesus, before Thy face I humbly kneel, and with the most fervent desire of my soul, I pray and beseech Thee to impress upon my heart lively sentiments of faith, hope and charity, true contrition for my sins and a firm purpose of amendment. With deep affection and grief of soul, I ponder within myself, mentally contemplating Thy five wounds, having before my eyes the words which David the Prophet spoke concerning Thee: "They have pierced my hands and my feet, they have numbered all my bones."

"A plenary indulgence is granted on each Friday of Lent and Passiontide to the faithful who, after Communion, piously recite the above prayer before an image of Christ crucified; on other days of the year the indulgence is partial."

—*Enchiridion of Indulgences,* No. 22

## An Act of Spiritual Communion

MY JESUS, I believe that You are in the Blessed Sacrament. I love You above all things, and I long for You in my soul. Since I cannot now receive You sacramentally, come at least spiritually into my heart. As though You have already come, I embrace You and unite myself entirely to You; never permit me to be separated from You.  —*Enchiridion of Indulgences*

". . . Make as many Spiritual Communions as possible, to supply for the many Sacramental Communions which are not made. One every quarter of an hour is not enough. Make them shorter, but more numerous."

—*Our Lord to Sr. Benigna Consolata* (d. 1916)

✝

## The Two Divine Promises

PROMISE: "Each priest who worthily offers the Holy Sacrifice of the Mass for 30 consecutive days and, in addition, makes the Stations of the Cross daily, will receive for himself, and another soul selected by him, the assurance of eternal salvation."

PROMISE: "Likewise, each individual who will receive Holy Communion worthily for 30 consecutive days, and will recite one Our Father and Hail Mary for the welfare of the Holy Catholic Church, will receive for himself and one other soul selected by him, the assurance of eternal salvation."

—*Words of Our Lord to a Polish soul*

*Litografia Uniao-Gaia*

Our Lord giving Holy Communion.
(Statue in the Carmel of Coimbra, convent of Sr. Lucy of Fatima.)

### THE SOUL AFTER HOLY COMMUNION

"After you have received Holy Communion, offer the Divine Wealth you then possess to pay the debt of souls . . . Souls that eat My flesh possess God, the Author of life and of life eternal. That is how they become My heaven. Nothing can compare with their beauty. The angels are in admiration and, as God is with them, they fall down in adoration. O souls, if you only knew your dignity! . . . Your soul is My heaven; every time you receive Me in Holy Communion, My grace augments both your dignity and your beauty."

—*Our Lord to Sr. Josefa Menendez*

# 𝔗𝔥𝔢 𝔖𝔞𝔠𝔯𝔢𝔡 𝔥𝔢𝔞𝔯𝔱 𝔬𝔣 𝔍𝔢𝔰𝔲𝔰

The Sacred Heart of Jesus appearing to St. Margaret Mary.
(Apparitions of 1673-1675).

## THE TWELVE GREAT PROMISES OF OUR LORD
## TO ST. MARGARET MARY
### FOR THOSE DEVOTED TO HIS SACRED HEART

1. I will give them all the graces necessary for their state of life.
2. I will establish peace in their families.
3. I will console them in all their troubles.
4. They shall find in My Heart an assured refuge during life and especially at the hour of death.
5. I will pour abundant blessings on all their undertakings.
6. Sinners shall find in My Heart the source of an infinite ocean of mercy.
7. Tepid souls shall become fervent.
8. Fervent souls shall speedily rise to great perfection.
9. I will bless the homes in which an image of My Heart shall be exposed and honored.
10. I will give to priests the power of touching the most hardened hearts.
11. Those who propagate this devotion shall have their names written in My Heart, never to be effaced.
12. The all-powerful love of My Heart will grant to all those who shall receive Communion on the *First Friday* of nine consecutive months the grace of final repentance; they shall not die under My displeasure, nor without receiving their Sacraments; My Heart shall be their assured refuge at that last hour.

✝

HEART of Jesus, Source of all consolation, have mercy on us.

HEART of Jesus, Delight of all the saints, have mercy on us.

## THE NINE FIRST FRIDAYS

This devotion consists in attending Holy Mass and receiving Holy Communion in reparation for those who do not receive Our Lord, who do not love Him and who wound Him by their sinful lives.

PROMISE: "I promise you, in the excessive mercy of My Heart, that My all-powerful love will grant to all those who communicate on the First Friday of nine consecutive months, the grace of final penitence; they shall not die in My disgrace, nor without receiving their Sacraments. My Divine Heart shall be their safe refuge in this last moment."     —*Our Lord to St. Margaret Mary*

✝

## THE FEAST OF THE SACRED HEART

This feast occurs on the Friday after the Feast of Corpus Christi. (Corpus Christi Sunday is the second Sunday after Pentecost.)

PROMISE: "I ask that the Friday after the Feast of Corpus Christi be set apart for a special feast to honor My Heart, by communicating on that day and making reparation to it by a solemn act, in order to make amends for the indignities which it has received during the time it has been exposed on altars. I promise you that My Heart shall expand itself to shed in abundance the influence of its divine love upon those who shall thus honor it and cause it to be honored."          —*Our Lord to St. Margaret Mary*

✝

MOST Sacred Heart of Jesus,<br>I place my trust in Thee!

## Efficacious Novena to the
## Sacred Heart of Jesus

*Padre Pio recited this novena prayer every day for all those
who requested his prayers.*

1. O MY JESUS, You have said: "Truly I
say to you, ask and it will be given you, seek
and you will find, knock and it will be opened
to you." Behold I knock, I seek, and I ask
for the grace of *(Here name your request)*.

*Our Father. Hail Mary. Glory be to the Father.*

Sacred Heart of Jesus, I place all my trust in You.


2. O MY JESUS, You have said: "Truly I
say to you, if you ask anything of the Father
in My name, He will give it to you." Behold,
in Your name, I ask the Father for the grace
of *(Here name your request)*.

*Our Father. Hail Mary. Glory be to the Father.*

Sacred Heart of Jesus, I place all my trust in You.

*(Continued on next page. . .)*

3. O MY JESUS, You have said: "Truly I say to you, heaven and earth will pass away, but My words will not pass away." Encouraged by Your infallible words, I now ask for the grace of *(Here name your request)*.

*Our Father. Hail Mary. Glory be to the Father.*

Sacred Heart of Jesus, I place all my trust in You.

### Let Us Pray

O Sacred Heart of Jesus, for Whom it is impossible not to have compassion on the afflicted, have pity on us miserable sinners and grant us the grace which we ask of You, through the Sorrowful and Immaculate Heart of Mary, Your tender Mother and ours.

*Hail, Holy Queen.*

St. Joseph, foster father of Jesus, pray for us.

✝

HEART of Jesus, rich unto all who call upon Thee, have mercy on us.

HEART of Jesus, salvation of those who hope in Thee, have mercy on us.

HOLY HOUR OF REPARATION

Our Lord instructed St. Margaret Mary: "You shall arise between eleven o'clock and the midnight hour, and remain prostrate with Me during the space of an hour, and so appease the divine anger by imploring mercy for sinners. Thus shall you assuage in some sort the bitterness I felt at that time because of the abandonment by My Apostles. . . for not having been able to watch with Me for the space of one hour."

(An hour of night adoration in the home, or a holy hour on the First Friday, would represent a generous act of love.)

✝

## Consecration to the Sacred Heart of Jesus

An act of consecration may be made in one's own words or by reciting any one of the many acts of consecration. The following was composed by Pope Leo XIII.  *(Annum Sacrum,* May, 1899.)

MOST sweet Jesus, Redeemer of the human race, look down upon us humbly prostrate before Your altar. We are Yours, and Yours we wish to be. But, to be more surely united with You, behold, each of us freely consecrates himself today to Your Most Sacred Heart.

Many, indeed, have never known You. Many, too, despising Your precepts, have rejected You. Have mercy on them all, most merciful Jesus, and draw them to Your Sacred Heart. Be King, O Lord, not only of the faithful who have never forsaken You, but also of the prodigal children who have abandoned You. Grant that they may quickly return to their Father's house, lest they die of wretchedness and hunger. Be King of those who are deceived by erroneous opinions, or whom discord keeps aloof, and call them back to the harbor of truth and unity of faith, so that soon there may be but one flock and one Shepherd.

Grant, O Lord, to Your Church, assurance of freedom and immunity from harm. Give peace and order to all nations, and make the earth resound from pole to pole with one cry: "Praise to the Divine Heart that wrought our salvation —to It be glory and honor forever!" Amen.

✝

JESUS meek and humble of heart, make our hearts like unto Thine.

MAY the Sacred Heart of Jesus be loved in every place.

# ~ 5 ~
# The Blessed Virgin Mary

## The Three Hail Marys
*A devotion promoted by St. Anthony of Padua,*
*St. Leonard of Port-Maurice and St. Alphonsus Liguori*

Our Lady requested the daily recitation of three Hail Marys, and she revealed the following to St. Mechtilde:

"The first Hail Mary will be in honor of God the Father, whose omnipotence raised my soul so high above every other creature that, after God, I have the greatest power in Heaven and on earth. In the hour of your death I will use that power of God the Father to keep any hostile power far from you.

"The second Hail Mary will be in honor of God the Son, who communicated His inscrutable wisdom to me...In the hour of your death I will fill your soul with the light of that wisdom so that all the darkness of ignorance and error will be dispelled.

"The third Hail Mary will be in honor of God the Holy Ghost, who filled my soul with the sweetness of His love and tenderness and mercy...In your last hour I will then change the bitterness of death into divine sweetness and delight."

PROMISE: During an apparition to St. Gertrude, the Blessed Mother promised, "To any soul who faithfully prays the Three Hail Marys I will appear at the hour of death in a splendor of beauty so extraordinary that it will fill the soul with heavenly consolation."

PRACTICE OF ST. LEONARD: St. Leonard often preached the devotion of the Three Hail Marys morning and evening in honor of Mary Immaculate, to obtain the grace of avoiding all mortal sin during the day or night. He assured his listeners: "Those who remain persistently faithful to this pious practice will most certainly receive the grace of eternal salvation."

PRACTICE OF ST. ALPHONSUS LIGUORI: The Saint suggested that the Three Hail Marys be said kneeling and that this ejaculation should be recited after each Hail Mary: "By thy pure and Immaculate Conception, O Mary, make my body pure and my soul holy."

The devotion of the Three Hail Marys was also promoted by Fr. John Baptist of Blois, who founded the Confraternity of the Three Hail Marys. Pope Leo XIII granted an indulgence to those who practiced the devotion and Pope Benedict XV raised the Confraternity to the rank of an Archconfraternity.

✝

BLESSED be the name of Mary,
Virgin and Mother.
—*The Divine Praises*

PROMISE: Ven. Mary of Agreda (1602-1665) heard a voice from the throne speaking in the person of the Father: "Our chosen one shall be called Mary, and this name is to be powerful and magnificent. Those that shall invoke it with devout affection shall receive most abundant graces; those that shall honor it and pronounce it with reverence shall be consoled and vivified, and will find in it the remedy of their evils, the treasures for their enrichment, the light which shall guide them to heaven. It shall be terrible against the power of hell, it shall crush the head of the serpent and it shall win glorious victories over the princes of hell." —*The Mystical City of God*

## ONE AVE MARIA

". . .One *Ave Maria* [Hail Mary] said without sensible fervor, but with a pure will in a time of aridity, has much more value in my sight than an entire Rosary recited in the midst of consolations." —*The Blessed Mother to Sr. Benigna Consolata Ferrero*

"The holy and learned Jesuit, Father Suarez, was so deeply aware of the value of the Angelic Salutation [Hail Mary] that he said that he would gladly give all his learning for the price of one Hail Mary that had been said properly."

—*St. Louis De Montfort*
*The Secret of the Rosary* (p. 48)

## A HUNDREDFOLD REWARD

"Both Saint Bernard and Saint Bonaventure say that the Queen of Heaven is certainly no less grateful and conscientious than gracious and well-mannered people of this world. Just as she excels in all other perfections, she surpasses us all in the virtue of gratitude; so she would never let us honor her with love and respect without repaying us one hundredfold. Saint Bonaventure says that Mary will greet us with grace if we greet her with the Hail Mary." —*The Secret of the Rosary* (p. 47)

The Annunciation

PROMISE: "Whoever shall devoutly recall to me the joy I felt upon uttering the words, 'Behold the handmaid of the Lord,' I will most truly show him that I am his mother, and unfailingly I will succor him." —*The Blessed Mother to St. Gertrude*

*The Blessed Virgin Mary*

# The Angelus

*The Angelus is traditionally recited morning (6:00 a.m.), noon and evening (6:00 p.m.) throughout the year except during Paschal time, when the Regina Coeli is recited instead. (See p. 118.)*

V. The Angel of the Lord declared unto Mary.

R. And she conceived of the Holy Spirit. *Hail Mary*, etc.

V. Behold the handmaid of the Lord.

R. Be it done unto me according to thy word. *Hail Mary*, etc.

V. And the Word was made Flesh.

R. And dwelt among us. *Hail Mary,* etc.

V. Pray for us, O holy Mother of God.

R. That we may be made worthy of the promises of Christ.

## Let Us Pray

Pour forth, we beseech Thee, O Lord, Thy grace into our hearts, that we to whom the Incarnation of Christ Thy Son was made known by the message of an angel, may by His Passion and Cross be brought to the glory of His Resurrection. Through the same Christ Our Lord. Amen.

Our Lady of Mt. Carmel

# The Brown Scapular
## of Our Lady of Mount Carmel

HISTORY AND PROMISES: During the last Fatima apparition (October 13, 1917), the Blessed Mother held in her hand a Brown Scapular while she presented herself as Our Lady of Mount Carmel. When asked why Our Lady held it, Sr. Lucia answered, "...because she wants everyone to wear the scapular...because it is our sign of consecration to her Immaculate Heart."

The Brown Scapular worn by people today is a miniature form of the large scapular which is part of the Carmelite habit; a large Carmelite scapular was presented by Our Lady to St. Simon

Stock, General of the Carmelite Order, about the year 1251. During this apparition, the Blessed Mother told him:

PROMISE: "This shall be to you and all Carmelites a privilege, that anyone who dies clothed in this shall not suffer eternal fire; and if wearing it they die, they shall be saved."

THE SABBATINE PRIVILEGE: During another apparition, this one to Pope John XXII (1316-1334), the Blessed Mother generously granted what is known as the Sabbatine Privilege: that those who fulfill certain conditions will be freed from Purgatory on the first Saturday after death. This promise was also mentioned in a bull issued on March 3, 1322 by Pope John XXII. It was Pope Paul V (1605-1621) who settled a controversy concerning the Privilege when he issued an official statement in which he gave priests permission to preach that the Blessed Virgin of Mt. Carmel ". . .will aid the souls of the Brothers and Sisters of the Confraternity of the Blessed Virgin of Mount Carmel after their death by her continual intercession, by her suffrages and merits and by her special protection, especially on the day of Saturday, which is the day especially dedicated by the Church to the same Blessed Virgin Mary. . ."

To receive the Scapular privileges one must be enrolled in the Brown Scapular. One should ask a priest to make this enrollment. (See page 127 for Enrollment ritual.)

The conditions for obtaining the Sabbatine Privilege are:

1. Wear the Brown Scapular faithfully.
2. Observe chastity according to one's state in life.
3. Recite the Little Office of the Blessed Virgin daily, or, with permission, substitute for this another pious work, e.g., the daily recitation of five decades of the Rosary. Any priest with faculties to hear confessions (this includes most priests) has the faculty to commute (change) this third requirement.

# The Miraculous Medal Prayer

O MARY, conceived without sin,
pray for us who have recourse to thee.

HISTORY: St. Catherine Labouré, of the Daughters of Charity, received visions of the Blessed Mother which were to result in the introduction of the Miraculous Medal. During the vision that took place on July 18, 1830, in the chapel of the mother-house near Paris, France, the Blessed Mother sat on the director's chair near the altar. After confiding certain matters to St. Catherine, she said, "Come to the foot of the altar; there graces will be shed upon all, great and little, who ask for them. Graces will be especially shed upon those who ask for them."

During the vision that occurred on November 27, 1830, the Blessed Mother stood with her hands outstretched, brilliant rays of light coming from rings on her fingers. Some rings gave off no rays, representing graces for which souls forget to ask. Our Lady's feet were crushing the head of the serpent. An oval framed the Blessed Mother, showing these words in letters of gold: "O Mary conceived without sin, pray for us who have recourse to thee."

PROMISE: Then a voice was heard to say: "Have a medal struck after this model. Those who wear it will receive great graces. They should wear it around the neck. Abundant graces will be given to those who wear it with confidence." The back of the medal was then revealed: a large M surmounted by a bar and a cross. Beneath the M were the hearts of Jesus and Mary, the one crowned with thorns, the other pierced with a sword. The whole was encircled with twelve stars.

The medal had originally been called the "medal of the Immaculate Conception," but so many remarkable graces and favors were soon granted through it that it quickly became known as the Miraculous Medal.

*Central Assoc. Mir. M., Germantown, Pa.*

The Miraculous Medal

## The Memorare

*Famous Prayer of St. Bernard of Clairvaux*

REMEMBER, O most gracious Virgin Mary, that never was it known that anyone who fled to thy protection, implored thy help or sought thy intercession was left unaided. Inspired with this confidence, I fly unto thee, O Virgin of virgins, my Mother. To thee do I come, before thee I kneel, sinful and sorrowful. O Mother of the Word Incarnate, despise not my petitions, but in thy clemency hear and answer them. Amen.

The Sorrowful and Immaculate Heart of Mary

# Sorrowful and Immaculate Heart of Mary, pray for us.

"The time is now ripe. I wish mankind to turn to the Sorrowful and Immaculate Heart of My Mother. Let this prayer be uttered by every soul. . . Let this prayer dictated by My love as a supreme succor be approved and indulgenced, no longer partially and for a small portion of My flock, but for the whole universe, so that it may spread as a refreshing and purifying balm of reparation that will appease My anger."

—*Our Lord to Berthe Petit* (1870–1943)

PROMISES: "This devotion to the Sorrowful and Immaculate Heart of My Mother will restore faith and hope to broken hearts and to ruined families; it will help to repair the destruction; it will sweeten sorrow. It will be a new strength for My Church, bringing souls, not only to confidence in My Heart, but also to abandonment to the Sorrowful Heart of My Mother."

—*Our Lord to Berthe Petit*

## Prayers in Honor of the Seven Dolors of the Blessed Virgin Mary
*Approved by Pope Pius VII in 1815*

V. O God, come to my assistance;
R. O Lord, make haste to help me.
V. Glory be to the Father, etc.
R. As it was in the beginning, etc.

1. I grieve for you, O Mary most sorrowful, in the affliction of your tender heart at the prophecy of the holy and aged Simeon. Dear Mother, by your heart so afflicted, obtain for me the virtue of humility and the gift of the holy fear of God. *Hail Mary,* etc.

2. I grieve for you, O Mary most sorrowful, in the anguish of your most affectionate heart during the flight into Egypt and your so-journ there. Dear Mother, by your heart so troubled, obtain for me the virtue of generosity, especially toward the poor, and the gift of piety. *Hail Mary,* etc.

3. I grieve for you, O Mary most sorrowful, in those anxieties which tried your troubled heart at the loss of your dear Jesus. Dear Mother, by your heart so full of anguish, obtain for me the virtue of chastity and the gift of knowledge. *Hail Mary,* etc.

4. I grieve for you, O Mary most sorrowful, in the consternation of your heart at meeting Jesus as He carried His Cross. Dear Mother, by your heart so troubled, obtain for me the virtue of patience and the gift of fortitude. *Hail Mary,* etc.

5. I grieve for you, O Mary most sorrowful, in the martyrdom which your generous heart endured in standing near Jesus in His agony. Dear Mother, by your afflicted heart, obtain for me the virtue of temperance and the gift of counsel. *Hail Mary,* etc.

6. I grieve for you, O Mary most sorrowful, in the wounding of your compassionate heart, when the side of Jesus was struck by the lance before His Body was removed from the Cross. Dear Mother, by your heart thus transfixed, obtain for me the virtue of fraternal charity and the gift of understanding. *Hail Mary,* etc.

7. I grieve for you, O Mary most sorrowful, for the pangs that wrenched your most loving heart at the burial of Jesus. Dear Mother, by your heart sunk in the bitterness of desolation, obtain for me the virtue of diligence and the gift of wisdom. *Hail Mary,* etc.

### Let Us Pray

Let intercession be made for us, we beseech You, O Lord Jesus Christ, now and at the hour of our death, before the throne of Your mercy, by the Blessed Virgin Mary, Your Mother, whose most holy soul was pierced by a sword of sorrow in the hour of Your bitter Passion. Through You, O Jesus Christ, Saviour of the world, Who with the Father and the Holy Ghost lives and reigns world without end. Amen.

Mother of Sorrows

## Four Special Graces Promised
## to those Devoted to the Dolors of Our Lady

PROMISES: According to St. Alphonsus Liguori, Our Lord revealed to St. Elizabeth of Hungary four special graces that are given to those who are devoted to the dolors of His holy Mother.

1. That those who before death invoke the Blessed Mother in the name of her sorrows, should obtain true repentance of all their sins.
2. That He would protect in their tribulations all who remember this devotion, and that He would protect them especially at the hour of death.
3. That He would impress upon their minds the remembrance of His Passion, and that they should have their reward for it in Heaven.
4. That He would commit such devout clients to the hands of Mary, so that she might obtain for these souls all the graces she wanted to lavish upon them.

✝

## Seven Promises to Those who Meditate
## on Our Lady's Tears and Dolors

PROMISES: According to St. Bridget of Sweden (1303-1373), the Blessed Virgin grants seven graces to the souls who honor her daily by saying seven *Hail Marys* while meditating on her tears and dolors:

1. "I will grant peace to their families."
2. "They will be enlightened about the divine Mysteries."
3. "I will console them in their pains and I will accompany them in their work."

4. "I will give them as much as they ask for as long as it does not oppose the adorable will of my divine Son or the sanctification of their souls."

5. "I will defend them in their spiritual battles with the infernal enemy and I will protect them at every instant of their lives."

6. "I will visibly help them at the moment of their death— they will see the face of their mother."

7. "I have obtained this grace from my divine Son, that those who propagate this devotion to my tears and dolors will be taken directly from this earthly life to eternal happiness, since all their sins will be forgiven and my Son will be their eternal consolation and joy."

The Sorrowful Mother beneath the Cross

Our Lady of Guadalupe

## Prayer to Our Lady of Guadalupe

HOLY Mary of Guadalupe, Mystical Rose, intercede for Holy Church, protect the Sovereign Pontiff, help all those who invoke you in their necessities; and since you are the ever Virgin Mary and Mother of the true God, obtain for us from your most holy Son the grace of keeping our faith, sweet hope in the midst of the bitterness of life, burning charity, and the precious gift of final perseverance. Amen.

## THE STORY OF OUR LADY OF GUADALUPE

On December 9, 1531, the Blessed Virgin appeared on Tepeyac Hill, near Mexico City, to a 57-year-old Christian Indian who was on his way to attend Holy Mass. Amid heavenly music and shining with light, the Blessed Mother addressed Juan Diego with the affectionate diminutives, "Juanito, Juan Dieguito." The Blessed Mother requested that a church be built in her honor, and during her fifth appearance she provided roses as proof for the local bishop that she had really appeared (it was wintertime), arranging them herself in Juan's cloak. When Juan opened his cloak in the presence of the Bishop, a miraculous image of Our Lady was found on the rude cactus-fiber cloth. The image is now on display in the Basilica in Mexico City. The preservation of the image and of the cloth, after more than 450 years, cannot be scientifically explained.

The words of Our Lady to Juan Diego demonstrate her care and compassion for those who approach her with simplicity:

PROMISES: "Hear and let it penetrate into your heart, my dear little son; let nothing discourage you, nothing depress you. Let nothing alter your heart or your countenance. Also, do not fear any illness or vexation, anxiety or pain. Am I not here who am your Mother? Are you not under my shadow and protection? Am I not your fountain of life? Are you not in the crossing of my arms? Is there anything else that you need?" "Understand, my dear son, that I am the ever Virgin Mother of the true God, in whom we live, the Creator and Maker of Heaven and earth. It is my urgent desire that a temple be built here to my honor where I shall spread my love, compassion, succor and protection. I am your merciful Mother and a loving Mother to your fellow men who love me and trust me and seek my aid. I will listen to their lamentations and give solace in all their sorrows and their sufferings."

*—Our Lady to Juan Diego*

## Pope Pius XII's Prayer
## to Our Lady of Guadalupe

HAIL, O Virgin of Guadalupe, Empress of America! Keep forever under your powerful patronage the purity and integrity of Our Holy Faith on the entire American continent. Amen.

It is suggested that three Hail Marys be recited—for North, Central and South America.

✝

## Our Lady of Grace
## *or* Our Lady of the Bowed Head

This picture of Our Lady of Grace was discovered at Rome about the year 1610 by the Ven. Dominic of Jesus and Mary (1559-1630), who later became the fifth General of the Discalced Carmelite Order. One evening, when Dominic was walking past an old house that was to be converted into a convent, an interior impulse attracted him to a heap of debris. After closely examining the rubbish, his eyes fell upon this oil painting, which was torn and covered with dirt. Grieved at seeing a picture of the Heavenly Mother in such a miserable condition, he took it to his cell and repaired it.

One night, while praying for a particular favor as he knelt before the holy image, he noticed that dust had settled upon it. While he was gently removing the dust, the face of Our Lady suddenly became animated. She smiled at Dominic and nodded her head in token of her gratitude. Dominic feared that he was the victim of a diabolical illusion, but the Queen of Heaven dispelled his uneasiness with the following words: "Fear not, my son, for your request is granted. It will be accomplished and will be part of the recompense that you are to receive for the love that you bear to my Divine Son and myself."

When Our Lady invited Dominic to make another request of her, he asked for the release of one of his benefactors from Purgatory. The Holy Virgin promised to grant this request if several Masses and good works were offered for the soul. Shortly afterward, the Blessed Mother appeared with the soul of the benefactor, who had been delivered from Purgatory.

PROMISE: The Blessed Mother then promised Dominic, "All those who implore my protection, devoutly honoring this picture, will obtain their petition, and will receive many graces. Moreover, I shall hearken in a special manner to the prayers that shall be addressed to me for the relief of the souls in Purgatory."

Since Dominic wanted others to venerate the image and receive the benefits of the Holy Mother's promises, he placed the picture in the Church of Santa Maria della Scala. Later it was moved to various countries. Now it can be found in the church of the Viennese Carmel.

Our Lady of the Bowed Head

# Our Lady of Confidence

### STORY OF THE PICTURE
### AND PROMISE OF OUR LADY

Venerated in Italy for over two hundred years, this picture has a long record of many extraordinary favors obtained through its veneration, especially by the seminarians of the Lateran Palace, Rome. A remarkable promise was made by Our Blessed Mother to the Ven. Clare Isabella Fornari (1697-1744), a Poor Clare nun of Todi, Italy. The Blessed Virgin promised the nun that she would grant a particular tenderness and devotion toward herself to everyone who venerates her image in the picture of Our Lady of Confidence. Combined with the aspiration, "My Mother, my Confidence," this devotion has proven especially efficacious.

Our Lady of Confidence

My Mother, my Confidence!

## ~ 6 ~

# 𝕿𝖍𝖊 𝕴𝖓𝖋𝖆𝖓𝖙 𝕵𝖊𝖘𝖚𝖘

## The Chaplet of the Infant Jesus

The chaplet includes three *Our Fathers* in honor of the Holy Family and 12 *Hail Marys* in memory of the 12 years of the childhood of Jesus.

With your heart filled with love and gratitude for all the Infant Jesus has accomplished for your salvation, devoutly recite His holy chaplet in the following manner. While meditating on the goodness of the Infant Jesus, whose image is portrayed on the medal, say:

D IVINE Infant Jesus, I adore Your Cross, and I accept all the crosses You will be pleased to send me. Adorable Trinity, I offer You, for the glory of the Holy Name of God, all the adorations of the Sacred Heart of the Holy Infant Jesus.

*On each of the three following beads, this invocation is said:*

A ND the Word was made flesh, and dwelt among us.

Follow each aspiration with an *Our Father* in honor of the Holy Family.

*On each of the 12 beads, recite the same aspiration:*

# And the Word was made flesh, and dwelt among us.

Follow each aspiration with a *Hail Mary* in honor of the 12 years of Our Lord's sacred infancy.

*In conclusion, recite the* Glory be to the Father *and the invocation:*

# Holy Infant Jesus, bless and protect us.

PROMISE: The devotion of the chaplet of the Holy Infant Jesus was revealed to the Ven. Sr. Margaret of the Blessed Sacrament, a Discalced Carmelite nun who died at Beaune, France on May 26, 1648. The Divine Infant made known to Sr. Margaret that He would grant special graces to those who practice this devotion. As a sign of His approval, He showed her the chaplet shining with supernatural light.

Chaplet of the Infant Jesus

# Novena to the Infant Jesus of Prague in Urgent Need

*(To be said for nine days or nine consecutive hours.)*

O JESUS, Who said, "Ask and you shall receive, seek and you shall find, knock and it shall be opened to you," through the intercession of Mary, Your most holy Mother, I knock, I seek, I ask that my prayer be granted. *(Mention your request.)*

O JESUS, Who said, "All that you ask of the Father in My Name He will grant you," through the intercession of Mary, Your most holy Mother, I humbly and urgently ask Your Father in Your Name that my prayer be granted. *(Mention your request.)*

O JESUS, Who said, "Heaven and earth shall pass away, but My word shall not pass," through the intercession of Mary, Your most holy Mother, I feel confident that my prayer will be granted. *(Mention your request.)*

HISTORY AND PROMISES: About the year 1628, the Discalced Carmelite Fathers of Prague received from Princess Polixena the statue of the Child Jesus which was to become world-famous. The princess presented the statue to the priests with the prophetic words, "I give you what I prize most highly in the world. As long as you venerate this image, you shall not want." Three years later the city of Prague was sacked by enemies of the Faith. The miraculous statue was seized and thrown carelessly into a heap of trash, and its hands were broken off during its fall. The statue was discovered later by Ven. Cyril of the Mother of God, O.C.D. (1590-1675). One day he was praying before the statue when he heard the words, "Have pity on Me and I will pity you. Give Me My hands and I will give you peace. *The more you honor Me, the more will I bless you.*" Veneration of the Infant Jesus has resulted in graces, blessings and miraculous healings.

Ven. Cyril of the Mother of God, O.C.D. wrote the original Prayer to the Miraculous Infant Jesus of Prague. (See following page.)

Original statue of the Infant Jesus of Prague

## Original Prayer of Ven. Cyril to the Miraculous Infant Jesus of Prague

JESUS, unto Thee I flee,
Through Thy Mother praying Thee
In my need to succor me.

Truly, I believe of Thee
God Thou art with strength to shield me;
Full of trust, I hope of Thee
Thou Thy grace wilt give to me.

All my heart I give to Thee,
Therefore, do my sins repent me;
From them breaking, I beseech Thee,
Jesus, from their bonds to free me.

Firm my purpose is to mend me;
Never more will I offend Thee.

Wholly unto Thee I give me,
Patiently to suffer for Thee,
Thee to serve eternally.
And my neighbor like to me
I will love for love of Thee.

Little Jesus, I beseech Thee,
In my need to succor me,
That with Joseph and Mary
And the angels, I may Thee
Once enjoy eternally. Amen.

# Prayer to be Said by a Sick Person

*(May be used for a novena)*

O MERCIFUL Infant Jesus! I know of Your miraculous deeds for the sick. How many diseases You cured during Your blessed life on earth, and how many venerators of Your Miraculous image ascribe to You their recovery and deliverance from most painful and hopeless maladies. I know, indeed, that a sinner like me has merited his sufferings and has no right to ask for favors. But in view of the innumerable graces and the miraculous cures granted even to the greatest sinners through the veneration of Your holy infancy, particularly in the miraculous statue of Prague or in representations of it, I exclaim with the greatest assurance: O most loving Infant Jesus, full of pity, You can cure me if You will! Do not hesitate, O Heavenly Physician, if it be Your will that I recover from this present illness; extend Your most holy hands, and by Your power take away all pain and infirmity, so that my recovery may be due, not to natural remedies, but to You alone. If, however, You in Your inscrutable wisdom have determined otherwise, then at least restore my soul to perfect health, and fill me with heavenly consolation and blessing, that I may be like You, O Jesus, in my sufferings, and may glorify Your providence until, at the death of my body, You bestow on me eternal life. Amen.

# 7

# The Passion of Our Lord

## Offering of the Bitterness of Our Lord's Passion

I OFFER to You, O Lord, all the bitterness of Your Passion, in reparation for the offenses committed against You.

PROMISE: Once when Jesus Christ appeared to St. Mechtilde, He spoke to her concerning His Passion, saying: "I make over to you all the bitterness of My Passion, that you may offer it to Me again, as though it were your own possession. And whoever shall do this shall receive double at My hand, and whenever he renews this offering he shall assuredly receive the double; and this is that hundredfold which a man receives in this life, and in the world to come, life everlasting."

✝

## Sighs of Love and Tears of Devotion

WITH heartfelt grief, I sigh while considering Your Holy Passion, O Lord, and I beg You to wound my heart with the arrow of Your love.

PROMISE: "Whenever anyone sighs toward Me with love in meditating on My Passion, it is as though he gently touched My wounds with a fresh-budding rose, and I wound his heart in return with the arrow of My Love. Moreover, if he sheds tears of devotion over My Passion, I will accept them as though he had suffered for Me."      —*Our Lord to St. Mechtilde*

# A Loving Gaze toward the Crucifix

PROMISE: After touching a crucifix devoutly, St. Gertrude learned that ". . .if anyone only looks at the image of the Cross of Jesus Christ with a holy intention, God rewards him with such goodness and mercy that he receives in his soul, as in a spotless mirror, an image which is so agreeable that the whole court of Heaven delights therein; and this serves to increase his eternal glory in the life to come in proportion as he has practiced this act of devotion in this life."

# The Five Holy Wounds

*Repeat any one of the following ejaculations five times in honor of the Five Holy Wounds of Our Lord:*

JESUS, Saviour of the world, have mercy on me. You to Whom nothing is impossible, bestow mercy to the wretched.

O CHRIST, Who by Your Cross has redeemed the world, hear us.

HAIL, Jesus, my loving Spouse. I salute You in the ineffable joys of Your divinity; I embrace You with the affection of all creatures, and I kiss the sacred wound of Your love.

THE LORD is my strength and my glory; He is my salvation.

PROMISE: Our Lord made known to St. Gertrude that if any one of these ejaculations is repeated five times in honor of the Five Wounds of the Lord, spiritually kissing the wounds devoutly, adding some prayers or good works, and offering them through the Heart of Jesus, they will be as acceptable to God as the most arduous devotion.

# The Rosary of the Holy Wounds

*On the crucifix and first three beads:*

O JESUS, Divine Redeemer, be merciful to us and to the whole world. Amen.

STRONG God, holy God, immortal God, have mercy on us and on the whole world. Amen.

GRACE and mercy, O my Jesus, during present dangers; cover us with Your Precious Blood. Amen.

ETERNAL Father, grant us mercy through the Blood of Jesus Christ, Your only Son; grant us mercy, we beseech You. Amen, Amen, Amen.

The following prayers, composed by Our Lord, are to be said using the rosary beads.

*On the large beads:*

V. Eternal Father, I offer You the Wounds of our Lord Jesus Christ.
R. To heal the wounds of our souls.

*On the small beads:*

V. My Jesus, pardon and mercy.
R. Through the merits of Your Holy Wounds.

HISTORY: This devotion to the Holy Wounds and the following promises were revealed by Our Lord to Sr. Mary Martha Chambon (1841-1907), of the Monastery of the Visitation of Chambery. The cause for her beatification was introduced in 1937.

## PROMISES OF OUR LORD FOR THOSE WHO PRACTICE THIS DEVOTION

1. At each word that you pronounce of the Chaplet of the Holy Wounds, I allow a drop of My Blood to fall upon the soul of a sinner.
2. Each time that you offer to My Father the merits of My divine Wounds, you win an immense fortune.
3. Souls that will have contemplated and honored My crown of thorns on earth, will be My crown of glory in Heaven!
4. I will grant all that is asked of Me through the invocation of My Holy Wounds. You will obtain everything, because it is through the merit of My Blood, which is of infinite price. With My Wounds and My Divine Heart, everything can be obtained.
5. From My Wounds proceed fruits of sanctity. As gold purified in the crucible becomes more beautiful, so you must put your soul and those of your companions into My sacred Wounds; there they will become perfected as gold in the furnace. You can always purify yourself in My Wounds.
6. My Wounds will repair yours. My Wounds will cover all your faults. Those who honor them will have a true knowledge of Jesus Christ. In meditation on them, you will always find a new love. My Wounds will cover all your sins.
7. Plunge your actions into My Wounds and they will be of value. All your actions, even the least, soaked in My Blood, will acquire by this alone an infinite merit and will please My Heart.

*(Continued on next page.)*

8. In offering My Wounds for the conversion of sinners, even though the sinners are not converted, you will have the same merit before God as if they were.

9. When you have some trouble, something to suffer, quickly place it in My Wounds, and the pain will be alleviated.

10. This aspiration must often be repeated near the sick: "My Jesus, pardon and mercy through the merits of Your Holy Wounds!" This prayer will solace soul and body.

11. A sinner who will say the following prayer will obtain conversion: "Eternal Father, I offer You the Wounds of our Lord Jesus Christ to heal those of our souls."

12. There will be no death for the soul that expires in My Holy Wounds; they give true life.

13. This chaplet is a counterpoise to My justice; it restrains My vengeance.

14. Those who pray with humility and who meditate on My Passion, will one day participate in the glory of My divine Wounds.

15. The more you will have contemplated My painful Wounds on this earth, the higher will be your contemplation of them glorious in Heaven.

16. The soul who during life has honored the Wounds of our Lord Jesus Christ and has offered them to the Eternal Father for the Souls in Purgatory, will be accompanied at the moment of death by the Holy Virgin and the angels; and Our Lord on the Cross, all brilliant in glory, will receive her and crown her.

17. The invocations of the Holy Wounds will obtain an incessant victory for the Church.

Crucifix used by St. Paul of the Cross, Founder of
the Passionist Order.

## PROMISES OF OUR LORD GIVEN TO ST. GERTRUDE FOR THOSE WHO HONOR HIS HOLY WOUNDS

One day as St. Gertrude was completing her prayers and
salutations in honor of the Wounds of the Saviour, her compassion was rewarded by a vision of Our Lord, on whose
Wounds rested golden roses. Our Lord said to her: "Behold,
I will appear to you in this refulgent form at the hour of your
death, and I will cover all your sins, and adorn you with a
glory like that with which you have adorned My Wounds by
your salutations. All who do so shall receive the like favor."

Our Lord crowned with thorns

"They placed upon His sacred head a cap made of plaited thorns to serve Him as a crown. This cap was woven of thorn branches and in such a manner that many of the hard and sharp thorns would penetrate into the skull, some of them to the ears and others to the eyes. Hence one of the greatest tortures suffered by the Lord was that of the crown of thorns.."

—*Ven. Mary of Agreda*
 *The Mystical City of God,* Bk. 6, chap. 20.

## O Sacred Head Surrounded

O SACRED Head surrounded
By Crown of piercing thorn!
O bleeding Head, so wounded,
Reviled and put to scorn!
Death's pallid hue comes o'er Thee,
The glow of life decays,
Yet angel hosts adore Thee
And tremble as they gaze.

I see Thy strength and vigor
All fading in the strife,
And death, with cruel rigor,
Bereaving Thee of life;
O agony and dying!
O love to sinners free!
Jesus, all grace supplying,
O turn Thy face on me!

In this Thy bitter Passion,
Good Shepherd, think of me,
With Thy most sweet compassion,
Unworthy though I be;
Beneath Thy Cross abiding,
Forever would I rest,
In Thy dear love confiding,
And with Thy presence blest.

—*St. Bernard of Clairvaux (1090-1153)*

## Crown of Thorns Prayer

DEAR Lord, I am grieved when I consider Your sad condition when You wore the Crown of Thorns upon Your holy head. I desire to withdraw the thorns by offering to the Eternal Father the merits of Your Wounds for the salvation of sinners. I wish to unite my actions to the merits of Your Most Holy Crown, so that they may gain many merits, as You have promised. Amen.

### WORDS OF OUR LORD TO SR. MARY MARTHA CHAMBON

During an apparition of Our Lord to Sr. Mary Martha Chambon, He appeared in a pitiful state, wearing the Crown of Thorns. Appealing for compassion, He said, "Behold Him whom you seek, and the condition in which He is! Look. . .withdraw the thorns from My head by offering to My Father the merits of My Wounds for sinners. . .Go, seek for souls!" While Sr. Mary Martha was contemplating the holy Crown, she saw rays of glory darting from each thorn.

"My Crown of Thorns caused Me more suffering than all My other wounds. . .It was My most intense suffering after the Garden of Olives."   —*Our Lord to Sr. Mary Martha Chambon*

PROMISE: "The Holy Crown is for the faithful soul a source of merit. . .The Crown of Thorns will merit for you a crown of glory. . .A single soul performing her actions in union with the merits of My Holy Crown may gain more than many others."                —*Our Lord to Sr. Mary Martha Chambon*

# St. Margaret Mary's 33 Adorations of Our Lord on the Cross

*(To be made on Fridays)*

HISTORY AND PROMISE: "One Friday during Holy Mass, I felt a great desire to honor the sufferings of my Crucified Spouse. He told me lovingly that He desired that, every Friday, I adore Him thirty-three times upon the Cross, the throne of His mercy...I was to offer these acts of adoration to the Eternal Father together with the sufferings of His Divine Son, to beg of Him the conversion of all hardened and faithless hearts who resist the impulse of His grace. He told me, moreover, that at the hour of death He will be favorable to those who have been faithful to this practice." —*Our Lord to St. Margaret Mary*

"These thirty-three acts of adoration of Our Lord on the Cross may be made anywhere on Fridays, and even while attending to one's ordinary work. They require no special attitude, formula or vocal prayer. A simple look of love and contrition, coming from the depths of our heart and sent up to our Crucified Lord is sufficient to express our adoration and our gratitude to Him. It is also an appeal to the Blessed Virgin to intercede with the Heavenly Father for the conversion of sinners."     —*Autobiography of St. Margaret Mary*

# The Stations of the Cross

*(See p. 120 for Suggested Short Prayers for Making the Stations.)*

To gain a plenary indulgence for making the Stations it is necessary to move from Station to Station, to meditate on the sufferings of Our Lord (no specific prayers are required), and to have the intention of gaining the indulgence. (Indulgences can always be applied to the Souls in Purgatory.)

Moreover, "To acquire a plenary indulgence, it is necessary to perform the work to which the indulgence is attached and to fulfill three conditions: sacramental Confession, Eucharistic Communion and prayer for the intentions of the Supreme Pontiff [e.g., one *Our Father* and one *Hail Mary*]. It is further required that all attachment to sin, even to venial sin, be absent."

—*Enchiridion of Indulgences,* No. 26

✝

PROMISES: These were given to Bro. Estanislao (1903-1927), a member of the Brothers of the Christian Schools at Bugedo. According to the Master of Novices, Bro. Estanislao was a privileged soul who received messages from Heaven. His spiritual director asked him to write the promises made by Our Lord to those who have devotion to the Way of the Cross. These promises and the Brother's virtues have been favorably recognized by confessors and theologians.

1. I will grant everything that is asked of Me with faith when making the Way of the Cross.
2. I promise eternal life to those who from time to time pray the Way of the Cross.
3. I will follow them everywhere in life, and I will help them especially at the hour of death.
4. Even if they have more sins than blades of grass in the fields and grains of sand in the sea, all of these sins will be erased

by the Way of the Cross. (This promise does not eliminate the obligation to confess all mortal sins, and this before receiving Holy Communion.)

5. Those who pray the Way of the Cross often will have a special glory in Heaven.

6. I will deliver them from Purgatory—indeed, if they go there at all—the first Tuesday or Friday after their death.

7. I will bless them at each Way of the Cross, and My blessing will follow them everywhere on earth and, after death, in Heaven for all eternity.

8. At the hour of death I will not permit the devil to tempt them; I will lift all power from him in order that they will repose tranquilly in My arms.

9. If they pray it with true love, I will make of each one of them a living ciborium in which it will please Me to pour My grace.

10. I will fix My eyes on those who pray the Way of the Cross often; My hands will always be open to protect them.

11. As I am nailed to the Cross, so also will I always be with those who honor Me in making the Way of the Cross frequently.

12. They will never be able to separate themselves from Me, for I will give them the grace never again to commit a mortal sin.

13. At the hour of death I will console them with My presence, and we will go together to Heaven. Death will be sweet to all those who have honored Me during their lives by praying the Way of the Cross.

14. My soul will be a protective shield for them, and will always help them whenever they have recourse to it.

✝

"Next to the Mass, the Way of the Cross is the most beneficial of all devotions for the Holy Souls in Purgatory."
                                    —*A Poor Soul to a privileged nun*

"Make the Stations of the Cross every day."
                                    —*Our Lord to Sr. Josefa Menendez*

Our Lord Jesus Christ

# 8

# The Precious Blood

## Purification Prayer
## of St. Mary Magdalen de Pazzi

ALMIGHTY Father, I place the Precious Blood of Jesus before my lips before I pray, that my prayers may be purified before they ascend to Your divine altar.

†

## The "Constant" Prayer
## of St. Catherine of Siena

PRECIOUS BLOOD, ocean of divine mercy:
  Flow upon us!
Precious Blood, most pure offering:
  Procure us every grace!
Precious Blood, hope and refuge of sinners:
  Atone for us!
Precious Blood, delight of holy souls:
  Draw us! Amen.

## Offering of the Precious Blood

ETERNAL FATHER, I offer You the Most Precious Blood of Jesus Christ in atonement for my sins, and in supplication for the holy souls in Purgatory and for the needs of holy Church.
—*The Raccolta*

## Precious Blood Prayer in Response to Requests from Our Lord

DEAR JESUS, moved by an impulse of love, and with purity of intention, I wish to cover my humble labors with Your merits and bathe them in the supernatural gold of Your Precious Blood. I desire to consecrate my life to the saving of souls and the extension of Your glory, and I beg the Heavenly Father for as many souls as You shed drops of Blood during Your Passion.

"I have many hidden souls who in their humble labors are very useful workers in My vineyard, for they are moved by love, and they know how to cover their deeds with supernatural gold by bathing them in My Blood...You should clothe your actions in My merits, bathe yourselves in My Blood, and consecrate your lives to the saving of souls and the extension of My glory." —*Our Lord to Sr. Josefa Menendez*

"Ask My Father for as many souls as I shed drops of Blood during My Passion." —*Our Lord to Sr. Mary of St. Peter*

# ~ 9 ~

# Love of God

J ESUS, Mary, I love You! Save souls!

WORDS OF OUR LORD: "It would be impossible to formulate a more perfect Act of Love in fewer words than: 'Jesus, Mary, I love You! Save souls!' It contains all: love for Me, love for My Mother Mary, and love for souls whom I came to redeem. This 'Act of Love' includes all souls: the souls in Purgatory, the innocent, the suffering, the sinful, the dying, and even your own poor soul."

"Do not lose time! Every 'Act of Love' means a soul!"

"One 'Jesus, Mary, I love You! Save souls!' repairs a thousand blasphemies!"

"What would you like to give your Mother Mary?. . .Offer her a continual 'Jesus, Mary, I love You! Save souls!' With that you will be giving her everything!"

"I do not demand heroic acts from you, but merely trifles; only they must be offered with all your heart!. . .Why is it that I do not permit you [Sr. Consolata] so many vocal prayers? It is because the 'Act of Love' is more fruitful."

"When you will have uttered your last 'Jesus, Mary, I love You! Save Souls!' I will gather it up and will convey it by means of your life's writings to millions of souls who, though they be sinners, will welcome it and will follow you in the simple way of trust and love, and in that way will love Me."

—*Our Lord to Sr. Maria Consolata Betrone*
*Poor Clare Capuchin (1903-1946)*

✝

## Offering of Love and Praise
*Variation of a Prayer Often Recited by St. Gerard Majella*

MY GOD, I make the intention of offering to You as many acts of love and praise as the Blessed Virgin, all the Saints and angels, as well as all the faithful on earth have ever made. I desire to love You as much as Jesus Christ loves You. I wish to renew these acts at every pulsation of my heart.

### Every Action an Act of Love

"I will teach you how to make every action of yours a special act of love dedicated to Me. In the past you have made only a general intention. Now you must make the intention specific before every act...A long formula is not needed for this. Before every act, before entering or leaving a room, or before any activity, simply say: 'Jesus,' or 'Jesu,' and I will accept it as a dedication."        —*Our Lord to a chosen soul*

### Acts of Love during Little Trials

"To suffer for My sake, you need not bear great physical, mental or spiritual crosses. Little annoyances, disappointments and discomforts can be offered to Me in the same manner as your duties. Simply say: 'Jesus' whenever you make an error, or are cold. I will accept the suffering as borne for My sake..."
—*Our Lord to a chosen soul*

## VARIOUS REVELATIONS OF DIVINE LOVE

"Whenever you kiss My image, I in turn kiss you; whenever you press My image to your heart, I in turn press you to My Heart; whenever you think of Me, I in turn think of you. Indeed, you are always in My thoughts, but at these times I think of you with a special love and devotion."

—*Our Lord to a chosen soul*

"When you eat or drink, think that you are giving Me that alleviation and do the same whenever you take pleasure in anything whatever." —*Our Lord to Sr. Josefa Menendez*

"Whoever offers Me the satisfaction of his corporal necessities, such as eating, drinking, sleeping, etc., saying in his heart or with his lips, 'Lord, I take this food' (or whatever it may be) 'in union with the love with which You performed the like actions when on earth, for the glory of Your Father and the salvation of men'. . .each time he makes his offering in union with My divine love, he presents Me with a strong shield to protect Me against the insults and outrages of sinners."

—*Our Lord to St. Gertrude*

"Everything I say to one of My children is for all of them. . .Each soul is My favorite. . .If only you knew My love for each one." —*Our Lord to Gabrielle Bossis (1874-1950)*

"From time to time during the day, repeat a little phrase such as: 'This is for You, my Jesus.' It will warm your heart and bring balm to Mine." —*Our Lord to Gabrielle Bossis*

"Do not believe in chance, but learn to see the hand of your Father, your friend—the one who never leaves you—in everything that happens." —*Our Lord to Gabrielle Bossis*

"Do not get the idea that it is the greatest number of prayers that touches your God. It is the way you speak to Him. Be irresistible in love, abandonment and humility."
—*Our Lord to Gabrielle Bossis*

"You must act as if Jesus were always visibly present to you in a natural way. . . Speak to Our Lord as to your most sincere and devoted friend. Neither do or say anything without consulting Him. Before every action, however trivial, or whatever you may have to do or say, ask His advice."
—*Recommendation of a soul in Purgatory to Sr. M. de L. C.*

"Think no longer about yourself, about your perfection, or how to attain sanctity, about your defects, or your present and future troubles. No, I will see to your sanctification. You must henceforth think only of Me and of souls; of Me to love, of souls to save."      —*Our Lord to Sr. Benigna Consolata Ferrero*

"When the evening of this life comes, we will be judged on love."                                    —*St. John of the Cross*

# Prayers of Reparation

## The Golden Arrow

MAY the most holy, most sacred, most adorable, most incomprehensible and unutterable Name of God be always praised, blessed, loved, adored and glorified in Heaven, on earth and under the earth, by all the creatures of God and by the Sacred Heart of Our Lord Jesus Christ in the most Holy Sacrament of the Altar. Amen.

PROMISE: This prayer was dictated by Our Lord to Sr. Mary of St. Peter, O.C.D., Discalced Carmelite nun of Tours, France (1816-1848). Opening His Heart to her, our Saviour complained of blasphemy, saying that this sin wounds His Divine Heart more grievously than all other sins, since it is like a "poisoned arrow." He also told her that the two sins which offend Him the most grievously are blasphemy and the profanation of Sunday. Our Lord called the above prayer the "Golden Arrow," saying that those who would recite it would pierce Him delightfully, and also heal those other wounds inflicted on Him by the malice of sinners. Sr. Mary of St. Peter saw, "streaming from the Sacred Heart of Jesus, delightfully wounded by this 'Golden Arrow,' torrents of graces for the conversion of sinners."

The Holy Face of Jesus
from the image on Veronica's veil.
(The veil is kept in St. Peter's Basilica, The Vatican.)

## Prayer to Reproduce
## The Image of God in Our Souls

I SALUTE You, I adore You and I love You, adorable Face of my beloved Jesus, as the noble stamp of the Divinity! Completely surrendering my soul to You, I most humbly beg You to stamp this seal upon us all, so that the image of God may once more be reproduced by its imprint in our souls. Amen.

Our Lord told Sr. Mary of St. Peter, O.C.D. on November 5, 1845, that the image of His Holy Face is like a stamp which imprints the image of God upon our souls.

## Holy Face Aspiration to be
## Recited Frequently during the Day

ETERNAL Father, we offer You the Holy Face of Jesus, covered with blood, sweat, dust and spittle, in reparation for the crimes of Communists, blasphemers, and for the profaners of the Holy Name and of the Holy Day of Sunday. Amen.

✝

"Oh, if you only knew what great merit you acquire by saying even once, 'Admirable is the Name of God,' in the spirit of reparation for blasphemy!" —*Our Lord to Sr. Mary of St. Peter*

## Offering of the Holy Face
## to Appease God's Justice
## and Draw down Mercy upon Us

ETERNAL Father, turn away Your angry gaze from all guilty people whose faces have become unsightly in Your eyes. Look instead upon the face of Your Beloved Son, for this is the Face of Him in whom You are well pleased. We now offer You this holy Face, covered with shame and disfigured by bloody bruises, in reparation for the crimes of our age, in order to appease Your anger, justly provoked against us. Because Your divine Son, our Redeemer, has taken upon His head all the sins of His people that they might be spared, we now beg of You, Eternal Father, to grant us mercy. Amen.

*—Archconfraternity of the Holy Face*

✝

## Offering of the Sacred Heart

*Dictated by Our Lord to Sr. Mary of St. Peter*

ETERNAL Father, look upon the Sacred Heart of Jesus which I offer to You as a vase, that it might receive the wine of Your Justice, so that in passing through this Holy Channel Your Justice may be changed for us into the Wine of Your Mercy!

PROMISES OF OUR LORD JESUS CHRIST
IN FAVOR OF THOSE WHO HONOR HIS HOLY FACE

1. "They shall receive in themselves, by the impression of My humanity, a bright irradiation of My divinity, and shall be so illuminated by it in their inmost souls that, by their likeness to My Face, they shall shine in eternal life with a brightness surpassing that of many others." *(Promise to St. Gertrude)*

2. "Those who embrace this work of reparation with true piety will not be lost, for I Myself will defend them before My Father and I will give them the Kingdom of Heaven. I will grant them the grace of final perseverance."

*(Promise to St. Mechtilde)*

*The following were made by Our Lord to Sr. Mary of St. Peter:*

3. "Our Lord promised me that He would imprint His divine likeness upon the souls of those who honor the features of His Face."

4. "By My Holy Face you will work wonders!"

5. "Through this Holy Face you will obtain the conversion of many sinners. Nothing that you ask in virtue of the Holy Face will be refused you. Oh, if you only knew how pleasing is the sight of My Face to My Father."

6. "Just as, in an earthly kingdom, money which is stamped with the picture of the sovereign or ruling executive of the country procures whatever one desires to purchase, so, likewise, in the Kingdom of Heaven, you shall obtain all that you desire by offering the coin of My precious humanity, which is My adorable Face."

7. "Our Lord assured me that all persons who would apply themselves to this Work of Reparation to His Holy Face would perform the same service in His behalf as that which the saintly Veronica had performed."

*(Continued on next page.)*

8. "I will give you My adorable Face, and each time that you present it to My Father, My mouth will be open to plead your cause."

9. "In proportion to the care you take in making reparation to My face, disfigured by blasphemies, I will take care of yours, disfigured by sin. I will imprint My image on it and render it as beautiful as when it was washed in the waters of Baptism."

10. "Then Our Lord promised me that all who defended His cause in the Work of Reparation, whether by their words, their prayers or by their writing, He would Himself defend before His Eternal Father, and that He would give them His Kingdom. Then it seemed to me that Our Lord urged me to extend this promise in His Name to His priests, who through a crusade of preaching would advance the cause of Reparation.

"As for His spouses who would strive to honor and wipe His Holy Face in a spirit of atoning for blasphemies, Our Lord promised that at their death He would purify the face of their souls by effacing the stains of sin, and that He would restore to them their original beauty."

✝

# BEHOLD, O God, our Protector, and look upon the Face of Thy Christ!

"I believe that God has great plans of showing mercy to souls by revealing to us the power of His adorable Countenance. In this priceless gift we possess an infallible means of appeasing the anger of the Eternal Father, irritated by blasphemers, because whenever we beg Him to cast a look upon the Face of His Divine Son, the rod falls from His hands."
                                        —*Sr. Mary of St. Peter*

## Prayer of St. Therese of Lisieux to the Holy Face of Jesus

O JESUS, Who in Your bitter Passion became "the most abject of men, a man of sorrows," I venerate Your sacred Face whereon there once shone the beauty and sweetness of the Godhead; but now it has become for me as if it were the face of a leper! Nevertheless, under those disfigured features I recognize Your infinite love, and I am consumed with the desire to love You and make You loved by all men. The tears which well up abundantly in Your sacred eyes appear to me as so many precious pearls that I love to gather up, in order to purchase the souls of poor sinners by means of their infinite value. O Jesus, Whose adorable Face ravishes my heart, I implore You to fix deep within me Your divine image and to set me on fire with Your love, that I may be found worthy to come to the contemplation of Your glorious Face in Heaven. Amen.

## Holy Face Prayer for Sinners
*by St. Therese of Lisieux*

E TERNAL Father, since You have given me for my inheritance the Adorable Face of Your Divine Son, I offer that Face to You and I beg You, in exchange for this *coin* of infinite value, to forget the ingratitude of souls dedicated to You and to pardon all poor sinners.

## ~ 11 ~

# The Divine Mercy

## Chaplet of The Divine Mercy

Using the rosary beads, recite: one *Our Father,* one *Hail Mary,* and one *I believe in God.*

On the Our Father beads say this prayer, which was given by Our Lord to Sr. Faustina (1905–1938):

ETERNAL Father, I offer You the Body and Blood, Soul and Divinity of Your dearly beloved Son, Our Lord Jesus Christ, in atonement for our sins and those of the whole world.

On the Hail Mary beads say:

FOR the sake of His sorrowful Passion, have mercy on us and on the whole world.

In conclusion, say three times:

HOLY God, Holy Mighty One, Holy Immortal One, have mercy on us and on the whole world.

PROMISES: Our Lord instructed Sr. Faustina: "Unceasingly recite this chaplet that I have taught you. Whoever will recite it will receive great mercy at the hour of death...Priests will recommend it to sinners as a last hope of salvation. Even the most hardened sinner, if he recites this chaplet even once, will receive grace from My infinite mercy...Oh, what great graces I will grant to souls who will recite this chaplet...By means of it you can ask and obtain anything, if what you ask for will be compatible with My will. I want the whole world to know My infinite mercy. I want to give unimaginable graces to those who trust in My mercy."

Sr. Faustina wrote in her diary: "The Lord told me to recite this chaplet for the nine days before the Feast of Mercy [the first Sunday after Easter]. It is to begin on Good Friday. Then He told me, 'By this novena I will grant every possible grace to souls.'"

✝

## The Feast of Mercy

Our Lord told Sr. Faustina that it is His will that a Feast of Mercy be officially established in the Church on the first Sunday after Easter. He said to Sr. Faustina, "This feast emerged from My most tender pity, and it is confirmed in the depths of My mercy...I desire that it be celebrated with great solemnity on the first Sunday after Easter...I desire that the Feast of Mercy be a refuge and shelter for all souls, and especially for poor sinners. The very depths of My tender mercy are open on that day..." Our Lord also said that on the Feast of Mercy "are opened all the divine floodgates through which graces flow."

PROMISES: "I will pour out a whole ocean of graces upon souls who will approach the fount of My mercy...The soul that will go to Confession, and [on the Feast of Mercy] receive Holy Communion, shall obtain complete forgiveness of sins and punishment...Let no soul fear to draw near to Me, even though its sins be as scarlet."

To avail oneself of this promise, Our Lord prescribes:

1. The reception of Holy Communion on that Sunday.

2. The reception of the Sacrament of Penance [within several days before or after the Sunday, in accord with the Church's present practice in the matter of gaining a plenary indulgence].

Moreover, Our Lord recommends:

1. The recitation of the Chaplet of the Divine Mercy for nine days preceding the Feast (beginning on Good Friday).

2. "On My Feast—on the Feast of Mercy—run through the whole world and lead souls that fainted away to the source of My mercy. I will heal and strengthen them."

3. "I desire that adoration take place here [in church] for the intention of imploring mercy for the world."

~

Our Lord also requested that Sr. Faustina prepare herself for the Feast of Mercy by making another novena, known as the "Novena of Mercy," beginning on Good Friday. Sr. Faustina's novena prayers for each of these nine days, along with other information about this devotion, are included in a booklet entitled *Devotion to the Divine Mercy.* This booklet is published by Marian Helpers Center, Stockbridge, Mass. 01263.

## The Hour of Great Mercy

*Two Suggested Prayers for Use*
*at 3 o'clock in the Afternoon*

YOU expired, Jesus, but the source of life gushed forth for souls and the ocean of mercy opened up for the whole world. O Fount of Life, unfathomable Divine Mercy, envelop the whole world and empty Yourself out upon us.

O BLOOD and water, Which gushed forth from the Heart of Jesus as a fount of mercy for us, I trust in You.

PROMISE: During a vision of the Divine Mercy devotion, Our Lord said to Sr. Faustina, "At three o'clock implore My mercy especially for sinners; and, if only for a brief moment, immerse yourself in My Passion, particularly in My abandonment at the moment of agony. This is the hour of great mercy for the whole world...In this hour I will refuse nothing to the soul that makes a request of Me in virtue of My Passion."

Later, He added, "...as often as you hear the clock strike the third hour, immerse yourself completely in My mercy, adoring and glorifying it; invoke its omnipotence for the whole world, and particularly for poor sinners; for at that moment mercy was opened wide for every soul. In this hour you can obtain everything for yourself and for others for the asking; it was the hour of grace for the whole world—mercy triumphed over justice."

Our Lord requested of Sr. Faustina the making of the Stations of the Cross in this hour, if possible. If not, He asked that she step into the chapel for a moment and adore His Heart full of mercy in the Blessed Sacrament. He continued, "Should you be unable to step into the chapel, immerse yourself in prayer there where you happen to be, if only for a very brief instant."

## VARIOUS REVELATIONS OF DIVINE MERCY

"When you go to Confession, know this, that I Myself am waiting for you in the confessional; I am only hidden by the priest, but I Myself act in the soul. Here the misery of the soul meets the God of Mercy. Tell souls that from this fount of mercy souls draw graces solely with the vessel of trust. If their trust is great there is no limit to My generosity."

*—Our Lord to Sr. Faustina*

"No soul will be justified unless it turns with confidence to My mercy...[Let] the greatest sinners place their trust in My mercy. They have the right before others to confidence in the abyss of My mercy...Graces are drawn from [the fount of] My mercy with one vessel only, and that is trust. The more a soul trusts, the more it will receive...I make Myself dependent upon your trust; if your trust will be great, then My generosity will know no limits...Sins of distrust wound Me most painfully."        *—Our Lord to Sr. Faustina*

PROMISE: "Souls who spread the honor of My mercy I shield through their entire life as a tender mother her infant, and at the hour of death I will not be a Judge for them, but the Merciful Saviour."        *—Our Lord to Sr. Faustina*

## ~ 12 ~

## 𝕿𝖍𝖊 𝕳𝖔𝖑𝖞 𝕽𝖔𝖘𝖆𝖗𝖞

## St. Louis De Montfort's Preparation for the Recitation of the Rosary

First, recite the prayer, *Come, Holy Ghost. (See p. 101).* Then say:

I UNITE myself with all the Saints in Heaven, and with all the just on earth; I unite myself with You, my Jesus, in order to praise Your holy Mother worthily and to praise You in her and by her. I renounce all the distractions that may come to me while I am saying this Rosary. Amen.

THE GREATNESS OF THE HOLY ROSARY

"When you say your Rosary the Angels rejoice, the Blessed Trinity delights in it, my Son finds joy in it too, and I myself am happier than you can possibly imagine. After the Holy Sacrifice of the Mass, there is nothing in the Church that I love as much as the Holy Rosary."    —*Our Lady to Blessed Alan*

✝

Our Lady asked for the daily Rosary each of the six times she appeared at Fatima.

79

## The Decade Prayer
*Requested by Our Lady of Fatima*

Our Lady said to Sr. Lucia of Fatima, "When you pray the Rosary, say after each decade:

O MY JESUS, forgive us our sins, save us from the fire of Hell, lead all souls to Heaven, especially those who are most in need of Thy mercy.

†

## The Fifteen Promises of Mary to Christians who Recite the Rosary
*Given to St. Dominic and Bl. Alan de la Roche*

1. Whoever shall faithfully serve me by the recitation of the Rosary, shall receive signal graces.
2. I promise my special protection and the greatest graces to all those who shall recite the Rosary.
3. The Rosary shall be a powerful armor against Hell; it will destroy vice, decrease sin and defeat heresies.
4. It will cause virtue and good works to flourish; it will obtain for souls the abundant mercy of God; it will withdraw the hearts of men from the love of the world and its vanities, and will lift them to the desire of eternal things. Oh, that souls would sanctify themselves by this means.
5. The soul which recommends itself to me by the recitation of the Rosary, shall not perish.
6. Whoever shall recite the Rosary devoutly, applying himself to the consideration of its sacred Mysteries, shall never be conquered by misfortune. God will not chastise him in His justice, he shall not perish by an unprovided death; if he

be just, he shall remain in the grace of God, and become worthy of eternal life.

7. Whoever shall have a true devotion for the Rosary shall not die without the Sacraments of the Church.

8. Those who are faithful to the recitation of the Rosary shall have, during their life and at their death, the light of God and the plenitude of His graces; at the moment of death they shall participate in the merits of the Saints in Paradise.

9. I shall deliver from Purgatory those who have been devoted to the Rosary.

10. The faithful children of the Rosary shall merit a high degree of glory in Heaven.

11. You shall obtain all you ask of me by the recitation of the Rosary.

12. All those who propagate the Holy Rosary shall be aided by me in their necessities.

13. I have obtained from my Divine Son that all the advocates of the Rosary shall have for intercessors the entire celestial court during their life and at the hour of death.

14. All who recite the Rosary are my sons, and brothers of my only Son, Jesus Christ.

15. Devotion of my Rosary is a great sign of predestination.

✝

# Rosary Novena
*also known as*
# The Irresistible Novena

This novena consists of reciting five decades of the Rosary each day for 27 days in petition; then immediately five decades each day for 27 days in thanksgiving, whether or not the request has been granted.

HISTORY AND PROMISE: The novena originated when Fortuna Agrelli, a girl of Naples, had suffered intense pain for 13 months. On February 16, 1884, she and her relatives began a novena of Rosaries for her recovery. Sitting on a high throne with the Infant Jesus on her lap, the Blessed Mother appeared to Fortuna on March 3. She held a rosary in her hand and was accompanied by St. Dominic and St. Catherine of Siena.

Fortuna petitioned Our Lady, "Queen of the Holy Rosary, be gracious to me, restore me to health. . ." The Blessed Virgin replied, ". . .You have invoked me by various titles and have always obtained favors from me. Now, since you have called me by the title so pleasing to me, 'Queen of the Holy Rosary,' I can no longer refuse the favor that you petition; for this name is most precious and dear to me. Make three novenas, and you will obtain all."

After Fortuna was cured, Our Lady appeared again. This time she said, "Whosoever desires to obtain favors from me should make three novenas of the prayers of the Rosary in petition and three novenas in thanksgiving."

The miracle is said to have made a very deep impression on Pope Leo XIII, who urged all Christians to love the Rosary and say it fervently.

## SEVEN GREAT BLESSINGS

In *The Secret of the Rosary* (p. 65), St. Louis De Montfort states: "The Rosary recited with meditation on the mysteries brings about the following marvelous results:

1. It gradually gives us a perfect knowledge of Jesus Christ;
2. it purifies our souls, washing away sin;
3. it gives us victory over all our enemies;
4. it makes it easy for us to practice virtue;
5. it sets us on fire with love of Our Blessed Lord;
6. it enriches us with graces and merits;
7. it supplies us with what is needed to pay all our debts to God and to our fellow men, and finally, it obtains all kinds of graces for us from Almighty God."

## THE ROSARY AND CONVERSION

"If you say the Rosary faithfully until death, I do assure you that, in spite of the gravity of your sins 'you shall receive a never fading crown of glory.' Even if you are on the brink of damnation, even if you have one foot in hell, even if you have sold your soul to the devil as sorcerers do who practise black magic, and even if you are a heretic as obstinate as a devil, sooner or later you will be converted and will amend your life and save your soul, if—and mark well what I say—if you say the Holy Rosary devoutly every day until death for the purpose of knowing the truth and obtaining contrition and pardon for your sins."     —*St. Louis De Montfort*
*The Secret of the Rosary* (p. 12)

✝

*See page 125 for How to Say the Rosary.*

## ~ 13 ~
## The Fatima Prayers

### The Pardon Prayer

My GOD, I believe, I adore, I trust and I love Thee! I ask pardon for those who do not believe, do not adore, do not trust and do not love Thee.

✝

### The Angel's Prayer

Most Holy Trinity, Father, Son and Holy Spirit, I adore Thee profoundly. I offer Thee the Most Precious Body, Blood, Soul and Divinity of Jesus Christ, present in all the tabernacles of the world, in reparation for the outrages, sacrileges and indifference by which He is offended. And through the infinite merits of His Most Sacred Heart, and the Immaculate Heart of Mary, I beg of Thee the conversion of poor sinners.

## Eucharist Prayer

O MOST Holy Trinity, I adore Thee! My God, my God, I love Thee in the Most Blessed Sacrament!

✝

## Sacrifice Prayer

Our Lady of Fatima said: Sacrifice yourselves for sinners, and say many times, especially whenever you make some sacrifice:

O JESUS, it is for love of Thee, for the conversion of sinners, and in reparation for the sins committed against the Immaculate Heart of Mary.

✝

## Rosary Decade Prayer

*To be said after the* Glory Be to the Father *following each decade of the Rosary.*

O MY JESUS, forgive us our sins, save us from the fire of Hell, lead all souls to Heaven, especially those who are most in need of Thy mercy.

*See page 129 for Fatima Promises.*

## THE FIVE FIRST SATURDAYS OF REPARATION

The Blessed Virgin appeared to Sr. Lucia in her convent at Pontevedra, Spain on December 10, 1925.

PROMISE: The Most Holy Virgin said, "...I promise to assist at the hour of death, with the graces necessary for salvation, all those who, on the first Saturday of five consecutive months, shall confess, receive Holy Communion, recite five decades of the Rosary, and keep me company for fifteen minutes while meditating on the fifteen Mysteries of the Rosary, with the intention of making reparation to me."

NOTE: Our Lord told Sr. Lucia that the Confession may be made any time during the eight days before or the eight days after the First Saturday. Moreover, He said, "It could be longer still, provided that, when they receive Me, they are in the state of grace and have the intention of making reparation to the Immaculate Heart of Mary."

# 14

# The Angels

## Prayer to the Queen of Angels to Defeat Satan

AUGUST Queen of Heaven! Sovereign mistress of the angels! Thou who from the beginning hast received from God the power and mission to crush the head of Satan, we humbly beseech thee to send thy holy legions, that under thy command and by thy power, they may pursue the evil spirits, encounter them on every side, resist their bold attacks and drive them into the abyss of eternal woe. Amen.

HISTORY: A Bernardine sister was shown the destruction caused by the devil throughout the world. The Blessed Virgin then told the nun that Hell had been let loose upon the earth and that the time had come for everyone to petition her, as Queen of the Angels, to send the heavenly legions to fight against the enemies of God and of men. Our Lady then communicated this prayer and requested that it be printed and distributed.

†

## St. Gertrude's Guardian Angel Prayer

O MOST holy angel of God, appointed by God to be my guardian, I give you thanks for all the benefits which you have ever bestowed on me in body and in soul. I praise and glorify you that you condescended to assist me with such patient fidelity, and to defend me against all the assaults of my enemies. Blessed be the hour in which you were assigned me for my guardian, my defender and my patron. In acknowledgment and return for all your loving ministries to me, I offer you the infinitely precious and noble heart of Jesus, and firmly purpose to obey you henceforward, and most faithfully to serve my God. Amen.

✝

## Prayer to St. Michael the Archangel

ST. MICHAEL the Archangel, defend us in battle; be our defense against the wickedness and snares of the devil. May God rebuke him, we humbly pray; and do thou, O Prince of the heavenly host, by the power of God, cast into Hell Satan and all the other evil spirits who prowl about the world seeking the ruin of souls. Amen.

HISTORY: After celebrating Holy Mass, Pope Leo XIII heard a conversation between Our Lord and Satan during which Satan threatened to harm the Church during a certain period of time. The Pope then realized that after this time, St. Michael would engage in mortal conflict with the devil in defense of the Church. The Pope then composed this prayer; for many years it was recited after Holy Mass in churches throughout the world.

✝

# Chaplet of St. Michael the Archangel

The Chaplet or Crown of St. Michael consists of nine groups of three beads, each group dedicated to a different choir of angels. A single bead separates each group of three. A medal representing the holy angels is attached to the Chaplet. In honor of each choir, the *Our Father* is recited on each separate bead and the *Hail Mary* on the small beads in each group of three. Each set begins with a prayer to one of the nine choirs of angels. (Leave the set of four beads until the end.)

Chaplet of St. Michael

*Begin with this invocation on the medal:*

V. Incline unto my aid, O God.
R. O Lord, make haste to help me.

*Glory be to the Father,* etc.

Then recite, beginning on the 1st separate bead:

1. By the intercession of St. Michael and the heavenly choir of the Seraphim, may it please God to make us worthy to receive into our hearts the fire of His perfect charity. Amen. *Our Father. 3 Hail Marys.*

2. By the intercession of St. Michael and the heavenly choir of the Cherubim, may God in His good pleasure grant us grace to abandon the ways of sin, and follow the path of Christian perfection. Amen. *Our Father. 3 Hail Marys.*

3. By the intercession of St. Michael and the sacred choir of the Thrones, may it please God to infuse into our hearts the spirit of true and sincere humility. Amen. *Our Father. 3 Hail Marys.*

4. By the intercession of St. Michael and the heavenly choir of the Dominions, may it please God to grant us grace to have dominion over our senses, and to correct our depraved passions. Amen. *Our Father. 3 Hail Marys.*

5. By the intercession of St. Michael and the heavenly choir of the Powers, may God vouchsafe to keep our souls from the wiles and temptations of the devil. Amen. *Our Father. 3 Hail Marys.*

6. By the intercession of St. Michael and the admirable heavenly Virtues, may it please God to keep us from falling into temptation, and may He deliver us from evil. Amen. *Our Father. 3 Hail Marys.*

7. By the intercession of St. Michael and the heavenly choir of the Principalities, may it please God to fill our souls with the spirit of true and sincere obedience. Amen. *Our Father. 3 Hail Marys.*

8. By the intercession of St. Michael and the heavenly choir of the Archangels, may it please God to grant us the gift of perseverance in the Faith, and in all good works, that we may be thereby enabled to attain the glory of Paradise. Amen. *Our Father. 3 Hail Marys.*

9. By the intercession of St. Michael and the heavenly choir of the Angels, may God vouchsafe to grant us their guardianship through this mortal life, and after death a happy entrance into the everlasting glory of Heaven. Amen. *Our Father. 3 Hail Marys.*

St. Michael the Archangel

An *Our Father* is recited on each of the four remaining beads. The first is in honor of St. Michael, the second in honor of St. Gabriel, the third in honor of St. Raphael, the fourth in honor of your guardian angel. Then recite the following:

### Anthem

O glorious prince, St. Michael, leader and commander of the heavenly host, guardian of the souls of men, conqueror of the rebel angels, steward of the palace of God, our worthy leader, endowed with holiness and power, deliver us from every evil. With full confidence we have recourse to you, that by your gracious protection we may be enabled to make progress every day in the faithful service of God.

V. Pray for us, most blessed Michael, Prince of the Church of Jesus Christ.

R. That we may be made worthy of His promises.

### Prayer

Almighty and everlasting God, Who by a prodigy of goodness and a merciful desire for the salvation of all men has appointed the most glorious archangel, St. Michael, prince of Your Church, make us worthy, we beseech You, to be delivered by his powerful protection from all our enemies, that none of them may harass us at the hour of death, but that we may be conducted by St. Michael into the august presence of Your Divine Majesty. This we beg through the merits of Jesus Christ our Lord. Amen.

PROMISES: Appearing to the Servant of God, Antonia d'Astonac, St. Michael revealed that he wished to be honored by nine salutations corresponding to the nine choirs of angels and that an Our Father and three Hail Marys should be said in honor of each of these nine choirs. The Archangel promised that whoever would practice this devotion in his honor would have, when approaching the Holy Table, an escort of nine angels, one chosen from each of the nine choirs. In addition, for the daily recital of these nine salutations he promised his continual assistance and that of all the holy angels during life, and after death, deliverance from Purgatory for themselves and their relations.

CAUTION: The book entitled *An Unpublished Manuscript on Purgatory* gives us these words revealed by a soul in Purgatory: "The promises of St. Michael are real, but you need not think that people who recite it out of routine and without any pains to become holy are taken out of Purgatory at once. That would be false. St. Michael does more than he promises, but he is not anxious to relieve those who are condemned to a long Purgatory. Certainly, as a reward for their devotion to the Archangel their sufferings are shortened, but as to delivering them at once, not so. I, who used to say it, can serve as an example of this. Immediate deliverance takes place only in the case of those who have worked with courage at their perfection and who have little to expiate in Purgatory. . .Those who promote the recitation of the chaplet deserve praise. It is this prayer that is the most efficacious in the present time of need."

✝

### Angel of God

ANGEL of God, my guardian dear,
To whom God's love entrusts me here;
Ever this day be at my side,
To light and guard, to rule and guide. Amen.

# 15

# The Poor Souls in Purgatory

## An Offering of the Holy Wounds and the Precious Blood

ETERNAL Father, I offer You the Holy Wounds of Your Son, and His Precious Blood, for the conversion of sinners and for the relief of the souls in Purgatory.

"When you offer My holy wounds for sinners, you must not forget to do so for the souls in Purgatory, as there are but few who think of their relief. . .

"The Holy Wounds are the treasure of treasures for the souls in Purgatory."     —*Our Lord to Sr. Mary Martha Chambon*

✝

St. Mary Magdalen de Pazzi learned from Our Lord to offer to the Eternal Father the Blood of His Divine Son. She made the offering 50 times a day, and in one of her ecstasies she saw a large number of sinners converted, and of souls delivered from Purgatory by this practice.

Jesus added, "Each time that a creature offers to My Father the Blood by which she has been redeemed, she offers Him a gift of infinite value."

—*Our Lord to St. Mary Magdalen de Pazzi*

## Eternal Rest

Eternal rest grant unto them, O Lord, and let perpetual light shine upon them. May they rest in peace. Amen.          —*The Raccolta*

✝

## Offering of Daily Actions

Eternal Father, by virtue of Your generosity and love, I ask that You accept all my actions, and that You multiply their value in favor of every soul in Purgatory. Through Christ Our Lord. Amen.

"If you make the intention, God will accept whatever you do for all the souls in Purgatory just as if applied to one particular soul."          —*A soul in Purgatory*
          (From *An Unpublished Manuscript on Purgatory*)

"It is more pleasing to God to perform all your actions in conscious union with Jesus and with a pure intention, on behalf of your deceased relatives, rather than to say many prayers for them."          —*A soul in Purgatory*
          (From *An Unpublished Manuscript on Purgatory*)

"Next to the Holy Mass, the Way of the Cross is the most beneficial devotion for the souls in Purgatory."
          —*A soul in Purgatory*
          (From *An Unpublished Manuscript on Purgatory*)

## Prayer to the Heart of Jesus

O GENTLEST Heart of Jesus, ever present in the Blessed Sacrament, ever consumed with burning love for the poor captive souls in Purgatory, have mercy on the soul of Your departed servant.

Be not severe in Your judgment, but let some drops of Your Precious Blood fall upon him (*or* her), and send, O merciful Saviour, Your angels to conduct him (*or* her) to a place of refreshment, light and peace. Amen.

## Into Paradise

MAY the Angels lead him into Paradise.

May the Martyrs receive him at his coming and take him to Jerusalem, the Holy City.

May the Choirs of the Angels receive him, and may he, with the once poor Lazarus, have rest everlasting. Amen.

—*The Roman Ritual*

MAY the souls of all the faithful departed, through the mercy of God, rest in peace. Amen.

# The Heroic Act in Favor of the Souls in Purgatory

O MY GOD! for Your greater glory, and to imitate as closely as possible the generous Heart of Jesus, my Redeemer, and also to testify my devotion to the Blessed Virgin, my Mother, who is also the Mother of the souls in Purgatory, I place in her hands all my satisfactory works, as well as the fruit of all those which may be offered for my intention after my death, that she may apply them to the souls in Purgatory according to her wisdom and good pleasure. Amen.

### EXPLANATION OF THE HEROIC ACT

This Heroic Act of charity is the completely unselfish offering to God of all the satisfactory value of one's prayers and good works—plus the value of any that may be offered for one after one's death—for the benefit of the souls in Purgatory, rather than for oneself. The "satisfactory value" of a good work is its value with regard to making up for our sins and reducing our stay in Purgatory. However, the "meritorious value" of our good works is inalienable, i.e., our merits, which give us a right to an increase of glory in Heaven, cannot be applied to anyone else. Moreover, a person who has made the Heroic Act may still pray for himself, friends and other intentions.

The Heroic Act is revocable at will and is not a vow. Its actual ratification depends on the will of God. By making this act with purity of intention, one is relying upon the mercy of God and the prayers of the Communion of Saints to assist his soul after death. The Heroic Act was approved and encouraged by Pope Benedict XIII (1724-1730).

## WORDS OF OUR LORD

After St. Gertrude made the Heroic Act, Our Lord appeared to her and said: "In order that you may know how agreeable your charity for the souls of the departed has been to Me, I remit to you now all the pains of Purgatory which you might have suffered; and as I have promised to return you a hundred for one, I will further increase your celestial glory abundantly, giving you a special recompense for the charity which you have exercised toward My beloved souls in Purgatory by renouncing in their favor your works of satisfaction."

## WORDS OF A POOR SOUL

Whereas the Heroic Act should be made without anticipating a reward, still we know that the Lord cannot be outdone in charity and mercy. In the revelations of the soul in Purgatory recorded in *An Unpublished Manuscript on Purgatory,* we are told that "The heroic act is very pleasing to God and of great help to the souls in Purgatory, and very helpful to the generous souls who make it. By giving up a part of their [satisfactory] merits they do not lose, but actually gain."

## Prayer for Deceased Parents

O GOD, Who has commanded us to honor our father and our mother, in Your mercy have pity on the souls of my father and mother, and forgive them their trespasses; and make me to see them again in the joy of everlasting brightness. Through Christ Our Lord. Amen.

*See also "Our Lady of the Bowed Head," p. 38, and "The Chaplet of St. Michael," p. 89, for other efficacious devotions for the Poor Souls.*

## ~ 16 ~
## 𝖁𝖆𝖗𝖎𝖔𝖚𝖘 𝕰𝖋𝖋𝖎𝖈𝖆𝖈𝖎𝖔𝖚𝖘 𝕻𝖗𝖆𝖞𝖊𝖗𝖘

## The Sign of the Cross

*This most fundamental prayer is used to begin and end one's prayers and to ward off the attacks of the devil.*

IN THE NAME of the Father, and of the Son, and of the Holy Spirit. Amen.

"When you make the Sign of the Cross, do it always with the interior spirit. The cross should be the distinctive sign of all your actions; this sign honors the Most Blessed Trinity."
—*Our Lord to Sr. Benigna Consolata*

✝

## A Prayer to Say when using Holy Water

BY this holy water and by Your Precious Blood, wash away all my sins, O Lord.

REFLECTION: Holy water is a sacramental whose use represents a cleansing of the soul. It is an act of faith and devotion to make the Sign of the Cross with holy water, as upon entering a church. Holy water is a constant reminder of our Baptism, and its devout use remits venial sin. It is also beneficial when used against the assaults of spiritual enemies.

## Come, Holy Ghost

COME, Holy Ghost, fill the hearts of Thy faithful, and kindle in them the fire of Thy love.

V. Send forth Thy Spirit, and they shall be created;

R. And Thou shalt renew the face of the earth.

### Let Us Pray

O God, Who hast taught the hearts of the faithful by the light of the Holy Spirit, grant that by the gift of the same Spirit we may be always truly wise, and ever rejoice in His consolation. Through Christ Our Lord. Amen.

✝

### St. Teresa on Holy Water

St. Teresa of Avila knew well the efficacy that God has bestowed upon holy water. She wrote, "From long experience I have learned that there is nothing like holy water to put devils to flight and prevent them from coming back again. They also flee from the cross, but return; so holy water must have great value."

# The Flower Prayers of St. Gertrude

### PRAYER TO JESUS

HAIL, vivifying gem of divine nobility! Hail, most loving Jesus, unfading flower of human dignity! You are my sovereign and only Good.

PROMISE: After reciting this prayer, St. Gertrude was visited by Our Lord, who told her: "Whosoever salutes Me, as you have done, in reparation for the blasphemies and outrages which are poured forth on Me throughout the world, when he is tempted at the hour of his death and accused by the demon, will be consoled by Me..."

### PRAYER TO THE BLESSED VIRGIN MARY

HAIL, White Lily of the ever-peaceful and glorious Trinity! Hail, Vermilion Rose, the delight of Heaven, of whom the King of Heaven was born, and by whose milk He was nourished! Do thou feed our souls by the effusions of your divine influences.

PROMISE: During an apparition of the Blessed Mother, St. Gertrude noted that the Holy Trinity was depicted under the form of a white lily with three petals. The Blessed Mother made it known that she would exert her influence with the Holy Trinity on behalf of those who saluted her as the White Lily of the Trinity and the Vermilion Rose of Heaven. She then added: "I will appear at the hour of death to those who salute me thus, in such glory that they will anticipate the very joys of Heaven."

St. Gertrude the Great. (Our Lord made several promises of spiritual benefits for those devoted to this saint. See *The Revelations of St. Gertrude,* chap. 20.)

## Blessed Be the Will of God

MAY the most just, the most high, the most lovable Will of God be in all things done, praised and magnified forever! Amen.

## Heaven's Prayers of Praise

"Holy, holy, holy, Lord God Almighty, Who was, and Who is, and Who is to come."

*—Apoc.* 4:8

"Worthy art Thou, O Lord our God, to receive glory, and honor, and power: because Thou hast created all things; and for Thy will they were, and have been created."

*—Apoc.* 4:11

"Worthy is the Lamb that was slain to receive power, and divinity, and wisdom, and strength, and honor, and glory, and benediction. . . .To Him that sitteth on the throne, and to the Lamb, benediction, and honor, and glory, and power, for ever and ever."

*—Apoc.* 5:12-13

"Salvation to our God, Who sitteth upon the throne, and to the Lamb. . .

"Amen. Benediction, and glory, and wisdom, and thanksgiving, honor, and power, and strength to our God for ever and ever. Amen."

*—Apoc.* 7:10,12

"Great and wonderful are Thy works, O Lord God Almighty; just and true are Thy ways, O King of ages. Who shall not fear Thee, O

Lord, and magnify Thy name? For Thou only art holy: for all nations shall come, and shall adore in Thy sight, because Thy judgments are manifest."                    —*Apoc.* 15:3-4

✝

## A Prayer to Redeem Lost Time

*by St. Teresa of Avila*

O MY GOD! Source of all mercy! I acknowledge Your sovereign power. While recalling the wasted years that are past, I believe that You, Lord, can in an instant turn this loss to gain. Miserable as I am, yet I firmly believe that You can do all things. Please restore to me the time lost, giving me Your grace, both now and in the future, that I may appear before You in "wedding garments." Amen.

✝

## St. Teresa's Bookmark

Let nothing disturb thee.
Let nothing affright thee.
All things are passing.
Patience obtains all things.
He who has God has everything.
God alone suffices.

## Novena to St. Joseph

O GLORIOUS St. Joseph, faithful follower of Jesus Christ, to you do we raise our hearts and hands, to implore your powerful intercession in obtaining from the benign Heart of Jesus all the helps and graces necessary for our spiritual and temporal welfare, particularly the grace of a happy death, and the special favor we now implore. *(Mention your petition. Then say the following seven times in honor of the seven sorrows and joys of St. Joseph.)*

O Glorious St. Joseph, through the love that you bore to Jesus Christ, and for the glory of His Holy Name, deign to hear our prayers and obtain for us our petitions. O Jesus, Mary and Joseph, come to our assistance. Amen.

"I do not remember even now that I have ever asked anything of him [St. Joseph] which he has failed to grant...To other saints the Lord seems to have given grace to succour us in some of our necessities, but of this glorious saint my experience is that he succours us in them all..."

—*Autobiography of St. Teresa of Avila*, chap. 6.

## A Prayer for Religious Vocations

O LORD, send workers for Your harvest, so that the commands of Your only-begotten Son may always be obeyed and His Sacrifice be everywhere renewed. Look with favor upon Your family, and ever increase its numbers. Enable it to lead its sons and daughters to the holiness to which they are called and to work for the salvation of others. Through Christ our Lord. Amen.

## Prayer for Priests

*This prayer is from the Diary of Sr. Mary Faustina Kowalska (1905-1938) of the Divine Mercy Devotion. (Her cause for canonization was introduced in 1981.)*

O MY JESUS, I beg You on behalf of the whole Church: Grant it love and the light of Your Spirit, and give power to the words of priests, so that hardened hearts might be brought to repentance and return to You.

Lord, give us holy priests; You Yourself maintain them in holiness. O divine and great High Priest, may the power of Your mercy accompany them everywhere and protect them from the devil's traps and snares, which are continually being set for the souls of priests.

May the power of Your mercy, O Lord, shatter and bring to naught all that might tarnish the sanctity of priests, for You can do all things. I ask You, Jesus, for a special blessing and for light for the priests before whom I will make my confessions throughout my lifetime. Amen.

## Prayer for Priests and Missionaries

*This prayer was received by Sr. Josefa Menendez from Our Lord, who said to her, "Repeat these words every day."*

My dear Jesus, by Your most loving Heart, I implore You to inflame with zeal for Your love and glory all the priests of the world, all missionaries, and those whose office it is to preach Your word. Inflamed with this zeal, may they snatch souls from the devil and lead them into the shelter of Your Heart, where they may glorify You forever. Amen.

✝

"If you say an Our Father to all the Saints, with the intention, were it possible, of saying one for each of the Saints, your intention is accepted by them as though you had really done so."
—*Our Lord to St. Gertrude*

✝

## A Prayer to Venerate Any Saint

Eternal Father, I wish to honor St. (*Name*), and I give You thanks for all the graces You have bestowed upon him (*her*). I ask You to please increase grace in my soul through the merits of this saint, and I commit the end of my life to him (*her*) by this special prayer, so that by virtue of Your goodness and promise, St. (*Name*) might be my advocate and provide whatever is needed at that hour. Amen.

PROMISE: "When you wish to honor any particular saint and give Me thanks for all the graces I have bestowed on that saint, I increase grace in your soul through the merits of that saint. When you commit the end of your life to any of the saints by special prayers, I appoint those saints to be your advocates and to provide whatever you need at that hour."

—*Our Lord to St. Gertrude*

✝

## Daily Our Father in honor of St. John the Evangelist

PROMISE: During a vision in which St. John the Evangelist appeared to St. Gertrude, Our Lord told her that the Apostle was appointed by Him to be her advocate in Heaven. Grateful for this favor, St. Gertrude said to Our Lord, "Teach me, my dear Lord, how I can show my gratitude to him." Our Lord answered: "If any person says a *Pater Noster* daily in honor of this Apostle, reminding him of the sweet fidelity with which his heart was filled when I taught this prayer, he will not fail to obtain the grace of persevering faithfully in virtue, even to the end of his life."

✝

## St. Augustine's Prayer to the Holy Spirit

BREATHE in me, O Holy Spirit, that my thoughts may all be holy. Act in me, O Holy Spirit, that my work, too, may be holy. Draw my heart, O Holy Spirit, that I love but what is holy. Strengthen me, O Holy Spirit, to defend all that is holy. Guard me, then, O Holy Spirit, that I always may be holy. Amen.

✝

## House Blessing

VISIT, we beg You, O Lord, this dwelling, and drive from it all the snares of the enemy. Let Your holy angels dwell herein, to keep us in peace; and let Your blessings be always upon us. Through Christ Our Lord. Amen.

## House Blessing in Verse

VISIT, Lord, this house of ours,
   Drive wicked foes away;
Let holy angels stay with us
   To keep the peace of day;
Let every blessing come to us
   And 'bide with us always. Amen.

# The Miraculous Novena of Grace
### March 4 - March 12 or November 25 - December 3

PRAYER TO ST. FRANCIS XAVIER
*Attributed to Father Marcello Mastrilli, S.J. (17th century).*

MOST amiable and most loving St. Francis Xavier, in union with thee I reverently adore the Divine Majesty. I rejoice exceedingly on account of the marvelous gifts which God bestowed upon thee. I thank God for the special graces He gave thee during thy life on earth and for the great glory that came to thee after thy death. I implore thee to obtain for me, through thy powerful intercession, the greatest of all blessings—that of living and dying in the state of grace. I also beg of thee to secure for me the special favor I ask in this novena. (*Here you may mention the grace, spiritual or temporal, that you wish to obtain.*)

In asking this favor I am fully resigned to the Divine Will. I pray and desire only to obtain that which is most conducive to the greater glory of God and the greater good of my soul.

V. Pray for us, St. Francis Xavier.
R. That we may be made worthy of the promises of Christ.

(*Continued on next page.*)

## Let Us Pray

O God, Who didst vouchsafe, by the preaching and miracles of St. Francis Xavier, to join unto Thy Church the nations of the Indies, grant, we beseech Thee, that we who reverence his glorious merits may also imitate his example, through Jesus Christ Our Lord. Amen.

Then add an *Our Father* and *Hail Mary*, three times, in memory of St. Francis Xavier's devotion to the Most Holy Trinity, and *Glory be to the Father* 10 times in thanksgiving for the graces received during his 10 years of apostleship.

HISTORY: The Novena of Grace, which begins March 4th and ends on the 12th, the day of the canonization of St. Francis Xavier, owes its origin to the Saint himself. At Naples, in December, 1633, Father Marcello Mastrilli, S.J. was at the point of death. The Saint appeared to him and, bidding him renew a vow he had made to labor in Japan, said:

PROMISE: "All those who implore my help daily for nine consecutive days, from the 4th to the 12th of March included, and worthily receive the Sacraments of Penance and the Holy Eucharist on one of the nine days, will experience my protection and may hope with entire assurance to obtain from God *any grace* they ask for the good of their souls and the glory of God."

The Father arose, instantly cured. So well has the Saint kept this promise that this devotion in his honor became universally known as the Novena of Grace. Its efficacy is not restricted to the dates mentioned. It may be made very appropriately from November 25 - December 3, the Feast of St. Francis Xavier. Though any prayers can be said in honor of the Saint, the foregoing are generally recommended.

—From *My Prayerbook*, by Fr. Lasance

# A Prayer for the Dying

O MOST merciful Jesus, lover of souls, I beseech You, by the agony of Your Most Sacred Heart, and by the sorrows of Your Immaculate Mother, wash clean in Your Blood the sinners of the whole world who are to die this day. Amen.

Heart of Jesus, once in agony, have mercy on the dying.

✝

"What sadness, My child, if you were to arrive [in Heaven] alone! Provide yourselves, all of you, with a cortege of companion souls saved because of your solicitude, whether they be in far-away missions or close to your home...If only your souls could each become one of a constellation led by you into the home of the Father of the heavenly family...Mention their names often to Me: your proteges, your unbelievers, your deaf-mutes. I will hide them beneath My seamless robe steeped in My Blood."　　　　　　　—*Our Lord to Gabrielle Bossis*

# 17

# Familiar Catholic Prayers

*(The following are familiar traditional Catholic prayers. Note that the recitation of many chaplets and other multi-part prayers includes the recitation of one or more of these prayers.)*

## Our Father

OUR FATHER, Who art in Heaven, hallowed be Thy Name. Thy kingdom come, Thy will be done on earth as it is in Heaven. Give us this day our daily bread, and forgive us our trespasses, as we forgive those who trespass against us. And lead us not into temptation, but deliver us from evil. Amen.

## Hail Mary

HAIL MARY, full of grace, the Lord is with thee; blessed art thou among women, and blessed is the fruit of thy womb, Jesus. Holy Mary, Mother of God, pray for us sinners, now and at the hour of our death. Amen.

## Glory Be

GLORY BE to the Father, and to the Son, and to the Holy Spirit. As it was in the beginning, is now, and ever shall be, world without end. Amen.

## The Apostles' Creed

I BELIEVE in God, the Father Almighty, Creator of heaven and earth; and in Jesus Christ, His only Son, our Lord; who was conceived by the Holy Ghost, born of the Virgin Mary, suffered under Pontius Pilate, was crucified, died, and was buried. He descended into hell; the third day He arose again from the dead; He ascended into Heaven, sitteth at the right hand of God, the Father Almighty; from thence He shall come to judge the living and the dead. I believe in the Holy Ghost, the Holy Catholic Church, the Communion of Saints, the forgiveness of sins, the resurrection of the body, and life everlasting. Amen.

## Hail, Holy Queen
## Salve Regina

HAIL, holy Queen, Mother of mercy, our life, our sweetness and our hope. To thee do we cry, poor banished children of Eve. To thee do we send up our sighs, mourning and weeping in this valley of tears. Turn then, most gracious advocate, thine eyes of mercy towards us. And after this our exile, show unto us the blessed Fruit of thy womb, Jesus. O clement, O loving, O sweet Virgin Mary.

V. Pray for us, O holy Mother of God.

R. That we may be made worthy of the promises of Christ.

## Act of Contrition

*It is well to begin the Rosary and any other prayers by purifying our souls with an act of contrition.*

O MY GOD, I am heartily sorry for having offended Thee, and I detest all my sins because I dread the loss of Heaven and the pains of Hell; but most of all because they offend Thee, my God, Who art all good and deserving of all my love. I firmly resolve, with the help of Thy grace, to confess my sins, to do penance, and to amend my life. Amen.

## Act of Faith

O MY GOD, I firmly believe that Thou art one God in Three Divine Persons, Father, Son and Holy Ghost. I believe that Thy Divine Son became man, and died for our sins, and that He will come to judge the living and the dead. I believe these and all the truths which the Holy Catholic Church teaches, because Thou hast revealed them, Who canst neither deceive nor be deceived.

## Act of Hope

O MY GOD, relying on Thy almighty power and infinite mercy and promises, I hope to obtain pardon of my sins, the help of Thy grace, and Life Everlasting, through the merits of Jesus Christ, my Lord and Redeemer.

## Act of Charity

O MY GOD, I love Thee above all things, with my whole heart and soul, because Thou art all-good and worthy of all love. I love my neighbor as myself for the love of Thee. I forgive all who have injured me, and ask pardon of all whom I have injured.

# The Regina Coeli

*This prayer is recited morning, noon and evening during Paschal Time (from Easter through the evening of the Saturday after Pentecost) instead of The Angelus. It is traditionally recited standing.*

V. Queen of Heaven, rejoice. Alleluia.

R. For He whom thou wast worthy to bear. Alleluia.

V. Has risen as He said. Alleluia.

R. Pray for us to God. Alleluia.

V. Rejoice and be glad, O Virgin Mary. Alleluia.

R. For the Lord is truly risen. Alleluia.

## Let Us Pray

O God, Who by the Resurrection of Thy Son, Our Lord Jesus Christ, hast been pleased to give joy to the whole world, grant, we beseech Thee, that through the intercession of the Virgin Mary, His Mother, we may attain the joys of eternal life. Through the same Christ Our Lord. Amen.

# 18

# Appendix

## Act of Consecration
## to the Immaculate Heart of Mary
### by St. Louis De Montfort

*This consecration is actually a renewal of baptismal promises and a consecration to Our Lord through the Blessed Virgin Mary. It is more than simply a prayer; by making this consecration a person embarks on a complete program of life, which St. Louis De Montfort calls a way of salvation and holiness which is short, easy, secure and perfect. St. Louis recommends a period (12 days plus three weeks) of prayers, readings and spiritual exercises in preparation for making this consecration. (This is explained in his spiritual classic,* True Devotion to Mary.)*

I, *(Name)*, a faithless sinner, renew and ratify today in thy hands, O Immaculate Mother, the vows of my Baptism; I renounce forever Satan, his pomps and works; and I give myself entirely to Jesus Christ, the Incarnate Wisdom, to carry my cross after Him all the days of my life, and to be more faithful to Him than I have ever been before.

In the presence of all the heavenly court I choose thee this day for my Mother and Mistress. I deliver and consecrate to thee, as thy slave, my body and soul, my goods, both interior and exterior, and even the value of all my good actions, past, present and future; leaving to thee the entire and full right of disposing of me, and all that belongs to me, without exception, according to thy good pleasure, for the greater glory of God, in time and in eternity. Amen.

✝

## Short Form of Consecration
*This consecration can be repeated often throughout the day.*

O MARY, my Queen and my Mother, remember I am all thine. Keep me and guard me as thy property and possession. Amen.

✝

## The Stations of the Cross
*Suggested Short Prayers for Making the Stations*

Begin by expressing sorrow for all the sins of your life and rejecting all attachment to sin. (See p. 58 for indulgences.) If possible, move from Station to Station. Say before *each* Station:

V. We adore Thee, O Christ, and we bless Thee;

R. Because by Thy holy Cross Thou hast redeemed the world.

*(Genuflect at the word "Because" and remain on one knee; arise after "redeemed the world.")*

### First Station
## JESUS IS CONDEMNED TO DEATH
It was for our sins, O Jesus, that You were condemned to suffer. Grant that we may detest our sins and, by this repentance, obtain Your mercy and pardon.

### Second Station
## JESUS IS BURDENED WITH THE CROSS
O Jesus, grant us, by virtue of Your Cross, that we may accept the difficulties of our state with meekness and cheerful submission. May we always be ready to take up our cross and follow You.

### Third Station
## JESUS FALLS THE FIRST TIME
O Jesus, it was for our sins that You bore the heavy burden of the Cross and fell under its weight. May the thought of Your sufferings make us watchful over ourselves and save us from falling into sin.

### Fourth Station
## JESUS MEETS HIS SORROWFUL MOTHER
O Jesus, by the compassion which you felt for Your Mother, have compassion on us and give us a share in her intercession. Our most afflicted Mother, intercede for us, that through the sufferings of Your Son, we may bear with courage the sorrows of this life.

*Fifth Station*
## SIMON OF CYRENE HELPS JESUS
## TO CARRY THE CROSS

O Jesus, just as Simon relieved You of Your burden, inspire us also to console You by our prayers of reparation and love.

*Sixth Station*
## VERONICA WIPES THE FACE OF JESUS

O Jesus, may the contemplation of Your Holy Face enkindle in our hearts a more fervent love for You, and may Your image be graven on our minds and souls until we are transformed into Your likeness.

*Seventh Station*
## JESUS FALLS A SECOND TIME

O Jesus, our repeated falls into sin have added to the burden which You carried for our redemption. As You are weakened by the weight of our sins, we are the cause of this second fall. Please give us the strength never to offend You again.

*Eighth Station*
## JESUS SPEAKS
## TO THE WOMEN OF JERUSALEM

O Jesus, just as You instructed the women of Jerusalem, please instruct us in the ways of virtue and help us to escape the dreadful judgments prepared for all who reject or neglect You in this life.

### Ninth Station
## JESUS FALLS THE THIRD TIME

O Lord Jesus! We entreat You, by the merits of this third most painful fall, to pardon our frequent relapses and our long continuance in sin. May the thought of Your sufferings grieve us and move us to make frequent acts of love and reparation.

### Tenth Station
## JESUS IS STRIPPED OF HIS GARMENTS

O Jesus, by the pain You suffered in having Your clothing torn from Your bleeding body, please strip us of all conceit and pride, and instruct us in the ways of humility, purity of intention and simplicity of heart.

### Eleventh Station
## JESUS IS NAILED TO THE CROSS

As You were nailed to the Cross, O Jesus, fasten our hearts there also, that they may be united to You until death.

### Twelfth Station
## JESUS DIES ON THE CROSS

O Jesus, we devoutly embrace the holy Cross whereon You loved us even unto death. We thank You for Your sacrifice, and we desire to love You as much as You love us.

*Thirteenth Station*
### JESUS IS LAID IN THE ARMS
### OF HIS HOLY MOTHER

We grieve with you, O Mary, for the sorrow you experienced as you examined the wounds on the body of your dear Son. By these sacred wounds may we obtain pardon and mercy for our sins.

*Fourteenth Station*
### JESUS IS LAID IN THE TOMB

O Jesus, someday our bodies will also be placed in a tomb. Freed from the bonds of this earth, may we then be received into Heaven by You and Your holy Mother, so that we may praise and love You for all eternity. Amen.

✝

# How to Say the Rosary

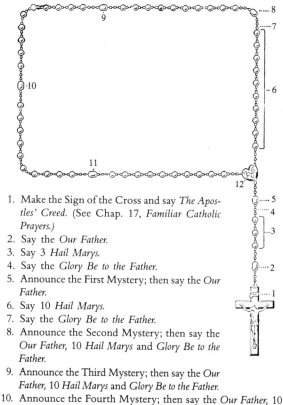

1. Make the Sign of the Cross and say *The Apostles' Creed.* (See Chap. 17, *Familiar Catholic Prayers.*)
2. Say the *Our Father.*
3. Say 3 *Hail Marys.*
4. Say the *Glory Be to the Father.*
5. Announce the First Mystery; then say the *Our Father.*
6. Say 10 *Hail Marys.*
7. Say the *Glory Be to the Father.*
8. Announce the Second Mystery; then say the *Our Father,* 10 *Hail Marys* and *Glory Be to the Father.*
9. Announce the Third Mystery; then say the *Our Father,* 10 *Hail Marys* and *Glory Be to the Father.*
10. Announce the Fourth Mystery; then say the *Our Father,* 10 *Hail Marys* and *Glory Be to the Father.*
11. Announce the Fifth Mystery; then say the *Our Father,* 10 *Hail Marys* and *Glory Be to the Father.*
12. Conclude by reciting the *Hail, Holy Queen.*

# The Mysteries of the Rosary
*To be meditated upon while praying the Rosary.*

### THE JOYFUL MYSTERIES
*Said on Mondays, Thursdays and the Sundays from the First Sunday of Advent until Lent.*

1st JOYFUL MYSTERY:  The Annunciation
2nd JOYFUL MYSTERY:  The Visitation
3rd JOYFUL MYSTERY:  The Nativity
4th JOYFUL MYSTERY:  The Presentation of Our Lord
5th JOYFUL MYSTERY:  The Finding of Our Lord in the Temple

### THE SORROWFUL MYSTERIES
*Said on Tuesdays, Fridays and daily during Lent.*

1st SORROWFUL MYSTERY:  The Agony in the Garden
2nd SORROWFUL MYSTERY:  The Scourging at the Pillar
3rd SORROWFUL MYSTERY:  The Crowning with Thorns
4th SORROWFUL MYSTERY:  The Carrying of the Cross
5th SORROWFUL MYSTERY:  The Crucifixion and Death of Our Lord on the Cross

### THE GLORIOUS MYSTERIES
*Said on Wednesdays, Saturdays and the Sundays from Easter until Advent.*

1st GLORIOUS MYSTERY:  The Resurrection of Our Lord
2nd GLORIOUS MYSTERY:  The Ascension of Our Lord
3rd GLORIOUS MYSTERY:  The Descent of the Holy Ghost upon the Apostles
4th GLORIOUS MYSTERY:  The Assumption of the Blessed Virgin Mary into Heaven
5th GLORIOUS MYSTERY:  The Coronation of Our Lady as Queen of Heaven and Earth

# Enrollment in the Brown Scapular

*Scapular Ritual for Priests*

Blessing and clothing with the Scapular of the Blessed Virgin Mary of Mt. Carmel enrolls the individual in the Scapular Confraternity (Confraternity of Our Lady of Mt. Carmel), a very large prayer organization. Scapular wearers share in the daily prayers of the Carmelite Order and the worldwide good works of the members of the Scapular Confraternity.

The ceremony of investing or "enrollment" in the Scapular and Confraternity is often performed after the reception of First Holy Communion. The following formula is used by the priest.

## THE SHORT FORMULA OF BLESSING AND ENROLLMENT

*Priest:* Show us, O Lord, Your mercy.

*All:* And grant us Your salvation.

*Priest:* O Lord, hear my prayer.

*All:* And let my cry come unto You.

*Priest:* The Lord be with you.

*All:* And with your spirit.

*Priest:* Let us pray:

*All:* O Lord Jesus Christ, Saviour of mankind, by Your right hand sanctify † these Scapulars (this Scapular) which Your servants will devoutly wear for the love of You and of Your Mother, the Blessed Virgin Mary of Mt. Carmel; so that by her intercession, they may be protected from the wickedness of the enemy and may persevere in Your grace until death, Who lives and reigns forever and ever.

*The priest now sprinkles the Scapulars with Holy Water, after which he places one on each person, saying:*

*Priest:* Receive this blessed Scapular and ask the Most Holy Virgin that, by her merits, it may be worn with no stain of sin and may protect you from all harm and bring you into everlasting life.

*All:* Amen.

*Priest:* By the power granted to me, I admit you to a share in all the spiritual works performed, with the merciful help of Jesus Christ, by the Religious of Mount Carmel, in the Name of the Father, and of the Son † and of the Holy Spirit.

*All:* Amen.

*Priest:* May Almighty God,

*All:* Creator of Heaven and earth, bless † those whom He has been pleased to receive into the Confraternity of the Blessed Virgin Mary of Mount Carmel. We beg her to crush the head of the ancient serpent in the hour of their death, and, in the end, to obtain for them a palm and the crown of Your everlasting inheritance. Through Christ Our Lord. Amen.

*The priest now sprinkles those enrolled with Holy Water.*

# Fatima Promises

## PROMISE OF THE GUARDIAN ANGEL OF PORTUGAL

"Make of everything you can a sacrifice, and offer it to God as an act of reparation for the sins by which He is offended, and in supplication for the conversion of sinners. You will thus draw down peace upon your country."

## PROMISES OF OUR LADY OF FATIMA

"Pray the Rosary every day, in order to obtain peace for the world, and the end of the war. . . . If what I say to you is done, many souls will be saved and there will be peace. . . . If my requests are heeded, Russia will be converted, and there will be peace. . . . In the end, my Immaculate Heart will triumph. The Holy Father will consecrate Russia to me, and she will be converted, and a period of peace will be granted to the world. In Portugal, the dogma of the Faith will always be preserved. . . . He [Jesus] wants to establish in the world devotion to my Immaculate Heart. I promise salvation to those who embrace it, and these souls will be loved by God, like flowers placed by me to adorn His throne. . . . The moment has come in which God asks the Holy Father, in union with all the Bishops of the world, to make the consecration of Russia to my Immaculate Heart, promising to save it by this means."

*—Words of Our Lady on various occasions*

## REQUESTS OF OUR LADY OF FATIMA

Our Lady's Fatima requests can be summed up thus: 1) the daily Rosary, 2) penance (particularly the fulfillment of one's daily duties) and sacrifices, 3) the Five First Saturdays, 4) devotion to the Immaculate Heart of Mary, 5) reparation. For more information, see the booklet entitled *Our Lady of Fatima's Peace Plan from Heaven,* available from TAN.

# The Green Scapular Prayer

IMMACULATE Heart of Mary, pray for us now and at the hour of our death.

HISTORY: The Green Scapular was revealed by Our Lady to Sister Justine Bisqueyburu, a novice in the Daughters of Charity, in 1840. Sister Justine understood that, through the Daughters of Charity, this new scapular would contribute to the conversion of souls, especially unbelievers, and obtain a happy death for them. The front of this scapular bears a picture of the Blessed Mother, her heart giving off abundant flames; the reverse shows her heart pierced by a sword and encircled by the words of the above prayer. There is no enrollment in the Green Scapular; it is sufficient that it be blessed by a priest. It may be worn, or it may be placed on the bed or personal effects or in the room of the person being prayed for. The prayer to be recited is that given above, which is printed on the Scapular. This prayer should be said daily, if not by the one receiving the Scapular, then by the one giving it. Graces are granted in proportion to the confidence accompanying the use of the Green Scapular. This fact was signified by the different kinds of rays which came from Our Lady's hands at her last apparition. Regarding the Green Scapular, Sister Justine wrote, "If it be given with confidence, there will be a great number of conversions." The Green Scapular was approved by Pope Pius IX in 1863 and 1870. Many spiritual and temporal favors, especially conversions, have been received through it.

*If you have enjoyed this book, consider making your next selection from among the following . . .*

Prices subject to change.

Practical Comm./Holy Scripture. *Knecht.* (Reg. 40.00) . 30.00
Sermons of St. Alphonsus Liguori for Every Sun. . . . . . 18.50
True Devotion to Mary. *St. Louis De Montfort* . . . . . . . 9.00
Religious Customs in the Family. *Weiser* . . . . . . . . . . . 10.00
Sermons of the Curé of Ars. *Vianney* . . . . . . . . . . . . . . 15.00
Revelations of St. Bridget of Sweden. *St. Bridget* . . . . . 4.50
St. Catherine Labouré of/Miraculous Medal. *Dirvin* . . . . 16.50
St. Therese, The Little Flower. *Beevers* . . . . . . . . . . . 7.50
Purgatory Explained. (pocket, unabr.) *Fr. Schouppe* . . . . 12.00
Prophecy for Today. *Edward Connor* . . . . . . . . . . . . . . . 7.50
What Will Hell Be Like? *St. Alphonsus Liguori* . . . . . . . 1.50
Saint Michael and the Angels. *Approved Sources* . . . . . . 9.00
Modern Saints—Their Lives & Faces. Book I. *Ball* . . . . 21.00
Our Lady of Fatima's Peace Plan from Heaven . . . . . . . . 1.00
Divine Favors Granted to St. Joseph. *Pere Binet* . . . . . . 7.50
Catechism of the Council of Trent. *McHugh/Callan*. . . . 27.50
Padre Pio—The Stigmatist. *Fr. Charles Carty* . . . . . . . 16.50
Fatima—The Great Sign. *Francis Johnston* . . . . . . . . . 12.00
The Incorruptibles. *Joan Carroll Cruz* . . . . . . . . . . . . . 16.50
St. Anthony—The Wonder Worker of Padua . . . . . . . . . . 7.00
The Holy Shroud & Four Visions. *Fr. O'Connell* . . . . . . 3.50
St. Martin de Porres. *Giuliana Cavallini* . . . . . . . . . . . 15.00
The Secret of the Rosary. *St. Louis De Montfort* . . . . . . 5.00
Confession of a Roman Catholic. *Paul Whitcomb* . . . . 2.50
The Catholic Church Has the Answer. *Whitcomb* . . . . . 2.50
I Wait for You. *Sr. Josefa Menendez* . . . . . . . . . . . . . . . 1.50
Words of Love. *Menendez, Betrone, etc.* . . . . . . . . . . . . 8.00
Little Lives of the Great Saints. *Murray* . . . . . . . . . . . . 20.00
Prayer—The Key to Salvation. *Fr. M. Müller.* . . . . . . . 9.00
Alexandrina—The Agony and the Glory. . . . . . . . . . . . . 7.00
Life of Blessed Margaret of Castello. *Fr. W. Bonniwell.* . 9.00
St. Francis of Paola. *Simi and Segreti.* . . . . . . . . . . . . . 9.00
Bible History of the Old and New Tests. *Schuster* . . . . . 16.50
Dialogue of St. Catherine of Siena . . . . . . . . . . . . . . . . . 12.50
Dolorous Passion of Our Lord. *Emmerich* . . . . . . . . . . . 18.00
Textual Concordance of the Holy Scriptures. PB. . . . . . . 35.00

***At your Bookdealer or direct from the Publisher.***
***Toll-Free 1-800-437-5876***        ***Fax 815-226-7770***
***Tel. 815-226-7777***        ***www.tanbooks.com***

Prices subject to change.

# ORDER FORM

Gentlemen:

Please send me _____ copies of **Prayers and Heavenly Promises**.

Name _____

Street _____

City _____

State ____ Zip _____ Phone _____

Enclosed is my payment of _____

Please charge my:
    ☐ VISA   ☐ MasterCard   ☐ Discover

Account number _____

Expiration date _____

Signature _____

All orders shipped promptly. U.S. and Canadian customers, please add shipping and handling on each order going to one address. (See over.) Illinois residents please add 7% sales tax. All foreign and Canadian customers please remit in U.S. funds payable thru a U.S. bank. Overseas customers please call or email us for exact freight. VISA, MasterCard and Discover welcome. For fastest service, phone, FAX or e-mail your order any time. FAX: 815-226-7770. You can also order thru our Website: www.tanbooks.com. Tel. Toll Free: 1-800-437-5876. Sales people are on duty Mon.-Fri.: 7 a.m.–8 p.m.; Sat.: 8 a.m.–6 p.m., Central Time. Leave a recorded order with your name and address, phone number and credit card number at any other time.

**TAN BOOKS AND PUBLISHERS, INC.**
**P.O. Box 424, Rockford, Illinois 61105**

St. Alphonsus Liguori tells us that we must pray in order to be saved. And there never was a greater need in the world for prayer than today. Yet many people in our generation have ceased to pray. Thus, this little prayerbook will fill a great need in helping people to pray and thereby to fulfill for themselves one of the essential requirements for salvation. Also, if this little book will gain wide distribution and will be widely used, it will help bring down many graces for our world, which seems to have lost for the most part the true knowledge of God. Therefore, this book can be of great benefit to others, as well as to ourselves. It is for these reasons that we are making it available at the lowest possible prices, that apostolic-minded people might better be able to place it in as many hands as possible. The issue is the salvation of souls and peace in the world.

## Quantity Discount

| | | | |
|---|---|---|---|
| 1 | copy | 6.00 | |
| 5 | copies | 3.00 each | 15.00 total |
| 10 | copies | 2.50 each | 25.00 total |
| 25 | copies | 2.25 each | 56.25 total |
| 50 | copies | 2.00 each | 100.00 total |
| 100 | copies | 1.75 each | 175.00 total |
| 500 | copies | 1.50 each | 750.00 total |
| 1,000 | copies | 1.40 each | 1,400.00 total |

*Prices subject to change.*

U.S. & CAN. POST/HDLG: If total order=$1-$10, add $3.00;
$10.01-$25, add $5.00; $25.01-$50, add $6.00;
$50.01-$75, add $7.00; $75.01-$150, add $8.00;
$150.01-up, add $10.00.

**TAN BOOKS AND PUBLISHERS, INC.**
**P.O. Box 424**
**Rockford, Illinois 61105**
**1-800-437-5876      www.tanbooks.com**